Up and Down the Ivory Tower

A.S.D

by

Larry Rodenstein

DORRANCE
PUBLISHING CO
EST. 1920
PITTSBURGH, PENNSYLVANIA 15238

Dorrance Publishing Co
585 Alpha Drive
Suite 103
Pittsburgh, PA 15238
Visit our website at *www.dorrancebookstore.com*

ISBN: 979-8-88683-318-8
eISBN: 979-8-88683-711-7

Dedicated to all the wonderful paraprofessionals
that worked with Keith during his home schooling.

Contents

My Childhood

When I was in first grade, I was out sick quite a bit with various infections. I was on antibiotics for a while. When I was out of school for long periods of time, my mother taught me the alphabet. In order to graduate first grade, the teacher said she would test me on the alphabet to see if I could recite it. I was able to do it and she said she would let me graduate to the second grade. When I was about eight years old, I had my tonsils and adenoids out. The doctors said that if I hadn't had my adenoids out, I might have gone deaf. I went to the Carney Hospital in Dorchester (part of Boston, Massachusetts) for the operation. I remember waking up in the bed in the hospital room and there was a cross above my bed at the head of my bed and I asked my mom what it was and she shushed me. Most of the nurses at the hospital were nuns. and she didn't want me to insult anyone with my ignorance.

I wanted to take Tap Dance, and Clarinet lessons, but my friends were going to Hebrew school. My mother told me that she could only afford one of the two, either tap dancing and clarinet lessons, or Hebrew school. I decided to go to Hebrew school because all my friends were going there. I remember almost nothing about Hebrew School first grade to sixth grade. I went to Hebrew school after public school Monday through Friday and Sunday mornings. The students had their own Sabbath service on Saturday mornings in a chapel downstairs in the building. I remember one Saturday morning the rascal in me had an Egg Bomb and I put it on the floor and crushed it. The whole chapel started smelling like rotten eggs. I was really afraid that they were going to catch me. The principal came in and I left the chair where I was sitting and left the chapel.

I grew up in a triple-decker multifamily house on a side street in Dorchester. My friends and I played in the schoolyard of my elementary school, which was about five houses down from where we lived. The swings were on one end and the rest was just asphalt and fences. We used to play pinky ball, which was like a form of baseball except we hit the ball with our hands from home plate and there was a diamond and we tried to run from home base to home base to hit a home run. Also, we played stickball in which one person would have a broomstick handle and the other person pitched the ball. The ball would go off the wall and back to the person who pitched if you missed it. The object was to try and hit a home run way over the pitcher's head. We didn't have any basketball courts. A friend of mine, Joey, had a basketball hoop in his backyard. It was nice to play one-on-one with Joey. I was pretty good at it. I could do this turnaround jump shot that was really cool.

In the summer they put the swings on the posts and they had counselors that would teach us how to do gimp and just hang out with us. Sometimes when we were playing in the schoolyard, the Irish kids would come down. It happened once or twice; they threw some rocks at us from over the fence. The older Jewish kids, the big boys, bigger and older than us, would harass us a lot. I had an older and bigger distant cousin, Jackie, who told me that if anybody hurt me, to let him know and he would come down and take care of them.

My friends and I were a little bit of rascals as a group, because we had no place to let off steam. Since, we would go almost directly from public school to Hebrew School. My friends' names were Chucky, Larry, Carl, Stevie, and Stuey. They were all Jewish kids that

I went to Hebrew school and public school with; oh yeah, one more friend was Vicky. He actually lived in the house behind our house. Vicky and I went downtown to Boston once. He wanted to steal some albums, so we went to Raymond's Department Store. He asked me to be the lookout for him. He ducked down below one of the counters and put some albums in a bag and all of a sudden some security guy came over to us and grabbed us both by the arms and took us into the Security office. He told us he was going to call the police. I said that it would be bad if we got a record. He was going to call our parents and Vicky started to cry. I was upset too, because I didn't want to get in trouble and get a record, so they held us at the office for a couple of hours. I said okay you can call. I think we went home and told our parents, but I can't remember for sure.

Another time, I had brought a squirt gun into the Hebrew school and from behind my back I squirted the principal in the face with the water and he didn't know where it was coming from. It was in a crowded hallway. The principal was also the sixth-grade teacher. One time, my friend Chucky and I were fooling around in the assembly hall while the principal was giving a lecture. He told us to go back to the classroom. So we went into the classroom and one of us had a firecracker and we put it in the pencil sharpener by the window and we lit it and just as we lit it the principal came in the room followed by the class of students and the firecracker went off and I started yelling that somebody threw a firecracker in through the window because the window was open a bit.

There was a husband and wife, elderly couple that owned a little store behind the school on the corner of one of the side streets. We used to go to the store and kind of terrorize the old couple by stealing stuff. It was a candy and soda store. It wasn't very nice of us, so I have to make amends on that, sometime.

I recall one time doing pull-ups on a pipe in the basement of the Hebrew school and the pipe broke. The water started coming out of it. They had to find the janitor. He lived in a house attached to the building and I guess he eventually shut the water off at the main valve. I think the basement flooded a bit because they had to call off school for a couple of days.

The district where I lived got red lined by some very wealthy real estate people and my folks decided to move before the area was going to turn African-American and they would lose value in their house. The real estate people bought the first few houses at market value and then sold them inexpensively to African-Americans. This caused the home prices to drop and the wealthy real estate people bought them and then sold them to the African-Americans at higher prices. They screwed the Jewish and the black people.

Most of my friends moved to Milton. My father's store in Roxbury had been broken into for cigarettes too many times, and he couldn't get theft insurance anymore for the store.

I was in the tenth grade when my father purchased a little supermarket in Brighton at the intersection of Sutherland Road and Commonwealth Avenue called Chansky's Market. The family he bought it from had stopped paying all of their suppliers for a while and instead were just putting the money away into safety deposit boxes. So, when my father purchased the store, he had to get a lawyer to make arrangements with the suppliers to see how much he would pay them. Some percentage on the dollar with maybe twenty-five cents on the dollar or something like that. I didn't know. I was too young to know what was going on.

We moved to Newton because my father's store was close to Newton. His store delivered to Brookline, Brighton, and Newton. I would go out with the driver and help deliver orders to the customers. I would also stock the shelves with Joe, (a fellow from the Quincy Naval yard who worked there part time). I also helped with the customers weighing the produce and putting prices on the bags. Whenever anybody asked my father a question, he would say, "Ask me no questions, I'll tell you no lies."

When I was younger, he never interacted with me much at all. I think he had post-traumatic stress syndrome from World War II. When he returned to his parents' house in Poland, it had been destroyed and his mother and father had been lined up in front of a hole and shot by the Germans into the hole. They were farmers, older and sick. His brother and his cousins ran up to the hills and the Russians gave them weapons to go back into the village with them and take the village back from the Germans. The Russians had a take-no-prisoners attitude.

We had some girl friends in Dorchester. One was Mindy Fleischman. I liked her a lot. I had a big crush on her, but she liked my friend Vicky better than me, and it really got me upset. So that was my first hurt feelings by a girl. I remember when Howie Smokler, one of our friends, got us some Tango from his uncle. His uncle was a bookie. I was in Latin School in the seventh grade and we were near the Boston State Hospital Grounds, in the backyard of some triple-decker multi-families, and we drank the Tango and then we walked up to Milton. I took the bus when we could to Mattapan Square and walked the rest of the way from Mattapan Square to Milton. We used to hang out with the Jewish girls there.

Tango removed my inhibitions about talking with the girls; it was a lot of fun. I remember my friend Chucky was dating Olivia and I liked her a lot. Olivia set me up with my first date, Amy Blank. I remember just putting my arm around her in the balcony at the movie theater, when we went out on a date, but I didn't really like her that much. Olivia is my closest lifelong friend. I've known her since I was twelve years old—fifty-eight years.

I recall one time walking from Mattapan to Milton and being stopped by a cop who asked me to walk a straight line. I tried to follow the crease in the concrete sidewalk and must have passed the sobriety test. I think that he was just trying to scare me.

Well, those are some of the things that I can recall from those early days of my life. When I was about twelve years old, I began studying my portion of the Torah that I would have to recite at my bar mitzvah.

On Friday nights, quite often we would go up to Mattapan Square and go to the movie theater there, named the Oriental Theater. The Irish kids would jump us and try to beat us up and try to prevent us from getting into our car and they tried to make us pay them for protection. They tried to make us fight with them. Most of them were from Catholic Memorial High School. One time I remember they lifted my coat over my head and beat me up. Those were the good old days. One time, I was going to bring in some of my friends that lived in Roxbury and they were going to come down and take care of the kids for us. Kenny Richardson, who lived in Roxbury dated Audrey Needle who was a good friend of Olivia's. Audrey ended up marrying Kenny and they had children.

For elementary school, I went to the William Bradford School, for kindergarten through third grade, and then I went to the Roger Williams School for secondary school. I completed grades four, five, and six at the Roger Williams School. I recall them wanting to test me to see if I was eligible for a double promotion. My mother told me not to take it, so when they asked me questions, I wrongfully answered one or two of them so that I wouldn't get the double promotion. I went to Boston Latin School from seventh grade until ninth.

When I was at Latin School, I worked at the RadioShack on Commonwealth Avenue across from Boston University. It was the main store and had a warehouse attached to it. I started out as a stock boy. I worked in the back room packaging things and stocking the shelves. I would go to the warehouse to get the items we needed for the store. I worked my way up to the parts counter as a Clerk. I learned how to read resistors and capacitors and get people the cartridges they wanted for their phonographs or their turntables. I also learned how to use the tube tester and how to provide people with new tubes when their old tubes were burnt out. I remember when I was still stocking shelves, I took a capacitor and charged it with a battery and I figured the person who bought that capacitor was going to get a heck of a shock. Now that I look back, it wasn't a very nice thing to do.

Chucky went to the University of Massachusetts at Amherst. I went to Huntington Prep for part of the summer before college. I met Kenny K. there. We all became friends again when I went to Northeastern. I liked Kenny a little better than Olivia and I didn't want to hurt his feelings, so I didn't try to date Olivia or anything. I think we might have gone out to McDonald's for lunch one day.

My Teenage Years

So for tenth, eleventh, and twelfth grades, I transferred to Newton public schools because my folks didn't want to pay the out-of-district cost for me to continue at Boston Latin School for the last three years. They were under the impression that the Newton Public Schools were very high quality. I was upset that we were moving to Newton, because most of my friends moved to Milton and I had heard that the people in Newton were snobs. I told my parents that I wasn't going to make any friends in Newton. It took me about a year to make a friend. I think Jerry G. was my first friend. He hooked me up with a group. I made a lot of friends at Newton South High School. The first day of school was kind of funny. At Latin School we had to wear a sports coat and tie.

When the teacher called on me I stood up and said, "Yes, sir." The teacher in my class wanted to introduce me to the other students because I was new in the city. The whole class cracked up laughing, so I knew that this was going to be a different animal. Newton South was a much more liberal school than Latin School. I had a small circle of friends: Jerry, Marty, Alan, Bruce, and Robbie. On the girls side, it was Carol and Bonnie (my high school girlfriend), Shelly, Barbara, and Patricia. These were my friends for the eleventh and twelfth grades. I believe that almost everyone had a car.

In eleventh grade, Jerry invited me to go with him to a Northeastern fraternity party on a Friday night. We went just to go try to snow job and pick up girls. When Bonnie, my girlfriend, heard about it, she got pissed off and got drunk and was in the back seat of a car making out with my neighbor Marty. I didn't do anything at the fraternity party. I told the girls that I was dancing with that I was a freshman. I just ruined the relationship with Bonnie. In the summer after I finished high school, I almost didn't get my high school diploma because I skipped gym so much.

At Latin School, in gym all we did was calisthenics—jumping jacks and push-ups and sit-ups and that sort of thing. Newton South had the horse that we had to do, the trampoline, climbing a rope, all sorts of equipment that I didn't like. I wasn't very good at it. I couldn't climb the rope up to the top of the ceiling and I didn't like the whole gymnastic program. So, I just kind of blew it off. The physical ed teacher at the end of the year said that he wasn't going to be able to give me a passing grade because I had skipped most of the classes all year. He said that the only way that he could give me a passing grade was if I joined the basketball team or ran after school. I agreed to run after school because I wasn't into any kind of organized sports at the time; that way I could get my high school diploma.

I skipped a lot of the twelfth grade of high school, maybe a quarter of the year. In terms of math class, my friend David H. would tell me when the math teacher was going to give an exam and I'd go in and just take the exams, because the mathematics that I had from Boston Latin School were much more advanced than Newton. It was just boring for me to go to the class, so I just went and took the exams and I did okay. Some of the other classes I went to, but I didn't do much either. All I really did was screw off. I don't know how I even got my high school diploma to be honest with you.

Once my friends came by in a car, when I was on the way to school and asked me if I wanted to go to the beach. I said, "Yes," cut my pants down to shorts and went to the beach with them.

We used to drink beer in the parking lot of the high school on the weekends. Once, the police came by to check us out. They confiscated the beer we had, like maybe three or four six-packs of beer in the back seat. They removed the beer and asked for our IDs and then they told us they would call our parents and let them know what we were doing, but all they did was take the beer, because our parents were never told about it.

The summer after high school, my friend Peter C. was going to open a Pottery Shop in Provincetown. He would throw the pottery at the back and I would be the sales clerk at the front. So, we rented a shack down in Provincetown for the two of us to stay at. It was rented for the summer so we had to pay the full amount. Then, his mother decided not to let us open the pottery shop. She wasn't going to pay the rent for the shop; so that fell through. I still had to pay the rent on the shack, so I went down and lived there. I helped to get some of the motels ready for the tourist season by painting and groundskeeping. At one motel, I helped an electrician pull some cables through some conduit. I also picked up laundry from people who stayed at the motel rooms and brought it to the laundry facility. I became friends with two guys at work at one of the motels. They lived next door to where my shack was and I called them Resemus and Rasmus. They went to Curry College in Milton. They were doing drugs, smoking marijuana and stuff. They asked me if I wanted to go to a party. They had some girlfriends whose parents had vacant houses there.

I remember one party we went to. We were drinking a lot of beer. I probably had six or eight beers maybe and was really tired from the beer. I was hungover and tired and so they asked me if I wanted to do some cocaine, and I said yeah sure; so we rolled a matchbook cover like a tube and then after snorting the coke within about five minutes

I was all refreshed and ready to party some more. It really scared me because I knew that's what all the actors in Hollywood do in order to keep partying. Those guys asked me if I wanted to do LSD.

I was really upset about Bonnie breaking up with me—the break-up we had from high school; I really had strong feelings for her. So, in that frame of mind, I took the LSD. I had a bad trip. I got paranoid. Resemus and Rasmus were strangers to me and I was paranoid about them. I didn't know whether to turn myself in to the police station and see if they could help me. I was afraid I'd get a record, so I decided not to. So, I walked home. I don't know how I got home. I could barely see in front of me. I got back to the shack and slept it off. We were kind of wild. After doing manual labor that summer, I decided that I would rather go to college.

During the summer, after I got out of high school, I had to take a course at Huntington Prep because I had skipped so much of my senior year, Northeastern wanted me to take a physics course. There were only three of us in the class at the beginning and then one fella had to drop out because his parents had passed away and he had to take care of his siblings. So, there were only two of us in the class. We really got one-on-one attention and the teacher was great. When I got into college, I was tops in my physics class, but there weren't any jobs as physicists at the time, so I decided to study mechanical engineering, which had a lot of physics in it. Everybody was cheating off me during the exams, but I didn't mind it.

My College Years

Northeastern had a five-year Cooperative Education program. There were Freshman, Sophomore, Midler, Junior, and Senior years. During those sessions, you would either be in school three or six months or at work three or six months.

After my Freshman year at Northeastern, I was supposed to work in my field. My Co-op advisor told me that he didn't have any jobs available.

My friend Jerry's father had a tool and die manufacturing company, and he dealt with a lot of Jewish businessmen. He told me that he could get me a job in a machine shop in Whitman called Alumitron and I took him up on it. I got a ride in with a European engineer, who Jerry's father had also gotten a job there. He worked in the air-conditioned office and I worked in the machine shop. The machine shop was unionized but, because I was only temporary, they let me work there. When the temperature got around 100 degrees, the people in the shop could go home. But I had to stay until the end of the day for my ride home. I learned how to use a Bridgeport milling machine, rotary saw, and some punch presses.

For my next co-op period, Jerry's father asked me if I'd like to get a job a little closer to home in an R&D department at a company called Stapler. I accepted that job and worked there for about three months before I had to go back to school. They made tape applicating machines for packaging so that the factories could identify the proper conveyor belt that the package would need to go on. It turned out that the company was owned by a lawyer and he was just trying to build it up so he could sell it. He moved it into a larger industrial building next door.

For my next co-op period, my co-op advisor told me that he had a good job for me at a company called Artisan Industries in Waltham, Massachusetts. I'd be an engineering assistant there. I interviewed there and got the job. The other company, Tapeler, called me and told me that they wanted me back. They offered me more money than Artisan, but I had already committed myself to work at Artisan. There were three engineers there: Eddie P., Art O., and Eddie B. I worked mostly for Eddie P. He was a Wentworth graduate and was quite good at designing things. Once, I remember when I found a better way to do something than he had designed, he agreed and changed the design to the way I told him would be better. I learned how to design pressure vessels and custom valves and flanges. They had a big rotary valve that was used in petroleum refineries and it would be custom made; so we would customize it for the customer. It was the size of a room, about 10' by 10'.

I worked there for a couple of co-op periods and then, since my cumulative average was so high, Northeastern said that I could join a group of guys and do my Master's Degree at the same time that I did my Bachelors. I had to write a master's thesis. There were five of us in the program: Malcolm, Tim P., Bob, Jimmy, and me. Jimmy was a Chinese guy who came to this country when he was about seven years old and he didn't go into kindergarten until he was seven because of not knowing English. So eventually, he aged out of the college deferment because of his age; so, he enlisted in the Navy. Otherwise he would have been drafted for four years. This way, all he had to do was a one- or two-year stint plus reserves afterwards. When he came back to college, he was a different person. He'd had straight As before going into the service, but now he was just trying to get by with Bs.

In my junior year, the recruiting department had companies come in to do interviews for jobs. The recruiting department trained us to do mock interviews so that we would be able to get jobs from the recruiters. I was offered about four jobs. One was Ingersoll Rand in Upstate New York. One was some kind of a nuclear reactor engineering company in New Jersey; one was Shell Oil Company down in Louisiana; and the other was Stone and Webster in Boston, a consulting firm designing and constructing nuclear power plants. Stone and Webster had about eleven to twelve nuclear power plant projects and it had never had a layoff in their sixty-plus years of business. I visited all of those company locations for interviews.

My Friends in College

My close friends in college were Tim M., Kenny K., Olivia M., Dave D., and Bill H. Dave and Bill were in Civil Engineering. Olivia was an English major I believe. Tim and I were in Mechanical Engineering.

Tim was my best friend in college. He and I were in a lot of the same classes, and boy did we have fun when we were bored. We had one calculus professor and he had us, at the end of his words he said 'sss; so, we knew he was gay and we made fun of him from the back of the class saying 'sss after he did.

One day, we were sitting in the last row of the class and as usual, he handed out the answers to our homework to be passed throughout the class. There was quite a stack of the answer sheets, when they reached us at the back of the classroom. I threw them out the window, I didn't realize that there was a lot of dins outside and the wind picked up all the papers and they were just flying all about the outside 2 sides of the class room windows. Tim and I were scared shitless that the professor would see, but he didn't.

Tim was a riot. We were in dirty Ernie's classroom together. He was an engineering professor who had designed the track at Northeastern. It didn't meet proper specifications for an indoor track for championship events. I think that's why they called him dirty Ernie.

So anyways, Tim and I were sitting there at the back of the classroom bored as hell and I took a look at what Tim was doing; he was drawing a cartoon of a bull dog peeing on a hydrant and I cracked up laughing. We had to hold it in and we barely could.

Well, I joined the engineers strike of the Vietnam War, but I wouldn't go marching outside because it was dangerous. You never knew when a policeman was going to hit you over the head with a billy club; even one of the reporters got hit in one of the phone booths with a billy club; so it was not good to be in protest marches.

I ended up with another feller, who I think was an English major doing a peaceful project. We went to Roxbury and there was a minister there who was looking to have a playground built for the kids instead of them selling and doing drugs. They would be able to participate in athletics. So the other guy and I met with the minister and I drew up the plans and we had an overlay of the area with a football field, baseball field, and a basketball court. The minister told us to bring the plans to Mayor White's office to get funding. We went up to Mayor White's office and met with Barney Frank, who at that time was Mayor White's right-hand man. He couldn't come out on his own because of his homosexuality. It was unacceptable at the time. Later he became a congressman. He told us to bring the plans to a construction company in Cambridge, show it to them and have them do the construction work.

After that I got out of it and went back to school. My professors had given me a couple of months off. They said they'd give me the grade that I had at the time of the strike. So, anyway I went back to school and buckled down and ended up in the accelerated program. All I learned how to do was take exams. I was working as a part-time night manager at Brighams and going to undergraduate school during the day and graduate school at night. I wasn't learning the material, but I was going to be more marketable when I got out. because I'd have a BS and MS at the same time. I was very good academically.

Tim was an auditory learner and he really didn't have to study much. I had to take notes and study my notes and study the textbooks. He would get Bs and I would get As, but he didn't have to study. He took it in stride.

When we got out of school, I kept in contact with Tim and he told me that he was taking the EIT ,(the engineer in training exam) and I was burned out on academics and I didn't know if I could pass the exam anyways, because all I had learned was how to take exams not really learn the material. After practicing as an engineer for six months, Tim was going to take the PE exam to be a Professional Engineer.

After college, he had an apartment in Framingham. Kenny and I used to go over once in a while and watch pornography and have some beer. The apartment was about halfway between his parents' house in Dorchester and his job at Norton in Worcester. He finally got engaged and they invited me to the wedding; he wanted me to be one of the ushers, but I didn't know if I'd be able to make it back for the wedding because I was working at Shell Oil Company in New Orleans.

Tim had studied ceramics. He really got into ceramics and I believe somebody was watching over him. He got a job working with ceramics brushes for Norton Industries. In school, he followed me around all over wherever I went. He was attached to me. He had a girlfriend and I pushed him towards her. His girlfriend, Marilyn, got straight As at Boston Teachers College, and I pushed him towards her because he needed a woman. He didn't need me. Tim eventually married her and had two daughters.

My Career

I took the job at Stone & Webster in Boston, because all my friends and family were in the Boston area. But about three months after I began working there, they lost about eleven of the thirteen nuclear power plant projects due to losing public financing. People didn't want to build nuclear power plants because they thought they were dangerous; so I just waited until it was my turn to be laid off. I began in the nuclear reactor plant group and was transferred to the pipes and fittings group. When I was in the nuclear reactor plant group, I sized and specified pumps and insulation for the plant. When they transferred me into the pipe and fittings group, I went about calculating how much pipe and how many fittings would be needed for the plant.

When the manager called me in to tell me I was being a member of the reduction in labor force, I said to him comically, "Well, at least my resume hadn't had time to collect any dust on the shelf." They were laying off a thousand engineers. They had hired a thousand new engineers and they would lay off a 1000. So I kind of panicked about it. A thousand engineers were going to be looking for jobs in Boston.

So, I decided on my second choice and called to see if the job was still available to me down in New Orleans at Shell Oil Company. The fellow I spoke to was the Division Mechanical Engineer and he said he would talk to his boss and see what he thought; he also at that time mentioned that they'd been losing a lot of engineers to the nuclear power industry and they were looking for engineers desperately. I got a call back in about an hour and he told me he had consulted with his boss and asked me when I could come down; the sooner the better. I told him I wanted to stay with my family for Thanksgiving and then I would come down immediately after.

John H. was the person who took me around when I first went to Shell for an interview. He met me at the airport when I came into town to interview for the job. I thought that it was going to be a glamorous job.

When I moved to New Orleans, John H. said to me, "I see that you didn't bring your girlfriend," and I tried not to think about it. He told me about this guy who worked at Shell that would go to bed with anything that had a dress on. John was very happily married.

The fellow who hired me was named Ken A. He was the Division Engineer for the Mechanical Engineering Department. He was considered a rising star within the organization. He had written a spiral bound booklet describing the very basics of Offshore Oil and Gas Production Facilities.

The Mechanical Engineering Division consisted of the Unit Engineers, the Chemical Engineering Section, the Civil Engineering Section, the Project Engineering Section, and specialists in Electrical Engineering, Compressors, and Piping and fittings.

I left Boston in a northeaster and when I arrived in New Orleans it was 95 percent humidity and 95 degrees. I was wearing a winter coat and I just immediately took my winter coat off. The first day at work I told them that I needed to go out and search for an apartment. They got me a rental car and I found an apartment on Lake Avenue. I looked at a map and it was near Lake Pontchartrain. I thought it would be nice to live by a lake. Soon enough I found out that the lake was polluted and you really couldn't swim there. The apartment I had was kind of depressing, it had cockroaches and wasn't very well kept. I lived there for a couple of years, and then my parents came down to visit me on their way to

California to see my mother's brother, my uncle, and they suggested I find a nicer place because the place I was living in was depressing.

So, I found a nicer place on Eden Avenue. It was like a Spanish architecture apartment complex, very nice. My next-door neighbor lived in the penthouse. He was a doctor. I became friends with him and a couple of times I had dinner at his place and we went out to eat with his lady friend.

I also made friends with one of my neighbors called Joey M. She was an alcoholic. She had been a debutante when she was younger. I'd go out and buy her a bottle of Pinch. She made dinner for me once in a while and she told me I had the manners of royalty. She fixed me up with a really nice neighbor, Patty L., who I later proposed to. She was Southern Baptist. My mother said that she wouldn't go to a church wedding and my sister told me the same. My mother recommended that I take her to a Rabbi. So we went to visit a rabbi and I realized how much I identified with Judaism due to my upbringing and going through six years of Hebrew School. I knew she would never convert because she was orthodox. So it split me up down the middle and I got mentally ill.

Patty had a friend named Mindy, who was Jewish and I told Patty that I wanted her to fix me up with Mindy. Mindy came to my apartment to talk to me and she gave me a really hard time because Patty was a good friend of hers.

A fellow who worked with me, Chuck, had been in the Air Force. He was a captain of helicopter maintenance. One of his helicopters had gone down and they attributed it to pilot error, but he wouldn't get promoted again. So after that, he left because once you don't get promoted you might as well resign and join the reserves; so that's what he did. He had been living in his own apartment and purchased a house.

The deal went foul and he had given notice at his apartment. I had a two-bedroom apartment and told him that he could stay in the second bedroom, if he paid half the rent. On the weekends, he would study the Air Force manuals because he wanted to eventually retire as a general. He had to take exams to work his way up to general and he would get a nice retirement pension from the federal government. He stayed with me about three months, then found another house to buy.

The Army Corp of Engineers would set regulations for safe practices. When new regulations became available he would find ways to get out of having to do them by finding loopholes.

The only two things that I know he did during the time he worked in the Mechanical Engineering Division were: (1) Designed and had a roof constructed over an area on one of his platforms so the maintenance people didn't get wet and (2) coordinated having a tank emptied and cleaned using a pump. Pumping everything from the tank into a barge. Then sending the barge ashore to dispose of the tank's ingredients into a pit. Whenever his supervisor called him into his office, he would detail him to death about what was going on in his unit and his supervisor liked it.

He had worked for the Ford Motor Company when he got out of college. He went to the University of Michigan and Henry Ford was his childhood hero. He and his father had built some 1935 Model T Ford trucks. He used to go to car shows and was so qualified that he was the judge in the show. He judged the cars to see which car had the most original parts on it. He used to call me "Stud" all the time. He and I went on camping trips together. We went over to Corpus Christi and saw the Alamo. It turned out to be a little shack with a movie screen telling the story of the "Last of the Alamo." We went out to the Texas Hill Country, which was just like little knolls. Not like the Blue Hills or anything in the Northeast. We went to Alabama and drove out and camped on Dauphin Island off the coast of Alabama. The island has a road that goes out to it.

Ken A. had gotten promoted to the head of Research and Development at Shell's Belaire Research Center in Houston.

When I was at Shell, they sent us to Houston to Shell's Bellaire Research Center for training. I think I went there three times for about two weeks each time. We were trained in geology, Drilling Engineering, Petroleum, and Production engineering. They gave us a survival course on how to survive jumping off a 50-foot-high platform without breaking our eardrums, also a survivalist session in terms of how you could stay in the water for a long time. You take your pants off and tie the legs in a knot and then force air into the legs. You then wrap it around yourself and make a life preserver out of it and you can do the same thing with your shirt and force air into it up to the sleeves and then you could wrap that around yourself and keep yourself afloat.

Some of the platform's had survival capsules. They could take about five or six people. They had a crane and a pulley that would drop the capsule into the water. The capsule had a motor that would allow you to get away from the platform.

Helicopters at that time were $100 per hour and they were piloted by ex-Vietnam pilots who could land on a dime. There were helipads on top of the platforms. We just walked down some stairs to get to the platform.

I was a Unit Engineer for offshore oil and gas production facilities. I was assigned to be the Unit Engineer for the Shoreline Unit. It had about seven platforms associated with it. My personal goal was to produce enough oil and gas to take pressure off of Israel, since it was around the time of the Arab oil embargo. I flew out on helicopters about every two weeks to check on projects that I was working on.

My job was to provide technical assistance to the unit. My section leader, Dan, told me to go out the first week and meet the two Maintenance Foremen and the Production Foreman and find out what they needed done on their platforms. One Maintenance Foreman's name was Alden V. and the other Maintenance Foreman's name was Red M. Alden was a prick and when he gave me the list of things he wanted me to work on, he said to me, "Are you ready to go back to Boston now?" I was just beginning to find out that a lot of the southerners didn't think the Civil War was over yet. Red was nicer to me; he didn't ask too much of me.

We had to get an AFE (Authority for Expenditure) approved by our Section Leaders, the Division Mechanical Engineer, and the Production Manager in the Operations Department for any projects we worked on. My first project was to have some pipelines constructed from a couple of wellheads on well jackets in the marshes onto the Halter Island production facility. It turned out that Alden had been the Maintenance Foreman when the Halter Island facility caught on fire and was destroyed. My section leader back then had to get a consultant, design, and reinstall a whole new facility there. He warned Alden to be careful lest it happen again. The rumor was that a switch had arced and lit some natural gas.

Well, I had to go down to the library to do research to find out how to lay pipelines through the marshes. I was still a bit of a novice at it and I didn't realize that you had to double up on things. I had sized the pipelines for the pressure that they would be exposed to including having aluminum sacrificial anodes every certain distance, so the pipeline wouldn't corrode. A couple of new well jackets would have to be installed because the old ones were falling apart and were unsafe. I didn't know how bad the marshes were and I copied the design of the original well jackets; wooden jackets with creosote-treated pilings to be driven down into the soil, the way the original ones were.

On one of the jackets, when the contractor went to drive the piles down into the soil, they just kept going deeper and deeper and deeper. I had made a big mistake. I should have put a steel well jacket with a concrete base out there and it would have worked out better.

Wayne P, had worked as a Unit Engineer and had also done a stint in the field on the platforms. He was considered a rising star and had been promoted into the Operations Department as the Production Manager for the Shoreline Unit. Wayne later implied that we should have installed steel well jackets with a concrete base so that they wouldn't be so rickety; I took it to heart.

Alden, had agreed to have the interconnecting piping from the lines that I had run to the top of the platform installed in the field. After the pipelines were run and brought up to the platform, I learned that Alden hadn't done what he had agreed to. I had sent the oil and gas separator to shore to get rebuilt. I heard that Wayne had gone out there for a couple of days on a weekend and had the lines connected to the oil and gas separator.

One day, Alden was making a repair on one of the tanks on the Eugene Island 128 facility. A Safety Engineer went out with me to observe them cutting out a rusted section of the tank with a torch and then welding a patch on. Well, the inside of the tank caught on fire. They had to put it out with a fire extinguisher. I told Alden that he had to coat the inside of the tank with the dry foam fire extinguisher substance before welding on the tank. They did that and successfully welded the patch on without having any more fires.

Another of the Unit Engineers was a guy named Mike, he was an MIT graduate. I used to see him at the bars at night of some of the clubs I went to. He was a little too rebellious of a guy. When we went to Houston one time for the Bel Air Research Center, he took a hotel suite at one of the fancy hotels. I was staying at a roach coach inn.

There was one other fellow named Jack. He was number one in his class in Chemical Engineering at Tulane and he was brilliant. Jack's father had worked at Shell in the drafting department and got laid off. This caused a divorce with Jack's parents, probably due to money issues. Jack wouldn't do much work for Shell because of what had happened to his father.

They sent Jack and me out to spend some time on a drilling rig. After a couple of days, we got bored of just sitting around watching as paleontologists onboard 24/7 watched for certain fossils to appear in the mud that would tell them whether they were about to strike oil or gas. The mudroom engineer would bring in samples of the mud at a certain frequency. The mud was circulated through the diamond drilling bit to keep it cool.

On about the first day of being on the rig, we got initiated by the guys spilling diesel on us from an upper deck. I thought it was kind of funny and just took it in stride.

As I stated, Jack and I got tired of sitting around watching men work and so we decided to help out when they were capping a well. We got on a huge pipe wrench that they used to tighten the lug nuts on the wellhead's flange and somebody's hands slid off the wrench,

The wrench slipped and cut the top of Jack's finger off. It was a foggy day and they couldn't get a helicopter out to bring Jack back to shore. We were about 150 miles offshore. Back then, the helicopters didn't have radar and so, they told us that we'd have to wait until the next day.

We called the hospital and they told us to put the finger in a glass of ice water and to keep the section that got cut off. In the morning we would fly back in and they would try to see if they could reattach the piece of finger that had been cut off. I sat up with Jack, I didn't want him to bleed to death. He had to go to the bathroom to pee and I asked him if he needed help with his zipper and he said, "No, that's okay." That became the joke of the week when I got back to work.

When I got back to the office, Lenny O., the new Division Mechanical Engineer, inquired as to what had happened and why I had left the drilling rig early. I told him what had transpired and that I'd seen what I had wanted to see and I wanted to make sure Jack was okay.

Lenny was from the business office and didn't know much of anything about real life engineering. He didn't even know how to read drawings. So, after a couple of fiascos, they transferred him to be the head of the construction department.

Wayne P. had been made the Division Mechanical Engineer after Lenny O. had been transferred. Wayne called me into his office once and asked me if I knew what a century was. I said, "Yes, it was 100 years."

He said, "Oh, I thought it was a thousand years."

I recall how I thought that Wayne had it in for me because of what happened at Halter Island. When Wayne became the new Division Mechanical Engineer, Chuck C. transferred to the Petroleum Engineering Department. He knew that it wasn't great if a former Operations Manager transferred to the Engineering Department. I think that Chuck was just going to wait it out in another department until Wayne was gone and then he'd transfer back to the Mechanical Engineering Department.

I had an opportunity to design an oil tank for a company. I had all the information that I would need to design it per the American

Society of Petroleum Engineers (ASPE) Standards. However, I thought that it would be a conflict of interest and I had a ton of work to do for Shell. If I had taken the contract for the tank, I probably would have ended up having my own consulting company, but I might have gotten fired from Shell.

Some of the Unit Engineers, after a couple of years as Unit Engineers, would go out to work on the platforms as Maintenance Foreman for six months or so, to get a real feel for what takes place on a platform.

There was a guy named Joe, who was also a Unit Engineer. He became an alcoholic within a couple of years. Well, most of the Unit Engineers were right out of college with no real experience. No one seemingly had a mentor to guide them; So, the stress would get to us. When Joe became an alcoholic, he left the job. I later heard that he had gotten a job as a draftsman somewhere. There was also a fellow named Mark, who also became an alcoholic. He left and I later heard that he had become a commercial aircraft pilot.

I also later learned that one of the engineers in the Project Engineering Section, Hugh, had put a sofa in his office. I heard that he got laid off later on. One of the other Engineers, Chris, was working on the Cognac Platform for 1000 feet of water. It was going to be the tallest platform ever installed.

He had a small motorboat and he, me, and Hugh went waterskiing on a meandering river a couple of times. All he asked was for me to chip in for gas. He and Hugh could slalom ski on a single oar, I still needed to ski on two legs on skis. I remember how strong Hugh's legs were because he could slalom ski on one oar for fifteen minutes or more. I was taught how to waterski in high school. A girlfriend named Sue G.'s parents had a summer house on a lake and they had a small motorboat.

I went to a party once at Robin M.'s. He was another of the Project Engineers. Rumor had it that he was buying up old oil and gas leases that were abandoned by oil companies because they weren't profitable enough for a larger oil company to continue producing from them.

At the party, someone told me about drinking a whole bottle of tequila to eat the worm at the bottom. I drank about half of it and then was as sick as a dog. I went out onto the front yard and I puked like there was no tomorrow.

When my new section leader was out on vacation, he asked me to sit in as the section leader. MIT graduate Mike B. and a couple of other people were in the section as Unit Engineers.

Mike had designed a safety system and I had to review the drawings before approving them.

It all looked good to me and I approved the project.

Mike had a vibrating pipe from the compressor on one of his platforms and instead of adding some support to it to make it stop vibrating, all he did was do the engineering calculations to simulate the vibration, but he didn't come up with a solution for it. All I would have done was to change where the supports were located so that it would prevent it from vibrating. Also, he was working on a flame arrestor for one of the heating units. I don't know whether he ever completed it.

After about a year with the Shoreline Unit, they transferred me to the Marlin Unit. The maintenance people there were much nicer. The Production Foreman was a great guy, very refined; he would do anything that I recommended.

One of my platforms needed a new surface safety system because the old one was in disrepair. I decided to design one and have it installed.

If there were any abnormal conditions on the facility, it would automatically shut down everything. If you needed to shut down the platform manually, there were valves available in convenient locations on the platform; especially the one at the stairs to the helipad.

One of my assignments was to come up with a remote device to shut down the platform from the helicopter. But I didn't know enough about electronics to design one, plus, I thought that it was a bit redundant anyway.

There was a fellow in the Mechanical Engineering Department, who had a lot of the piping on the platforms, in the dangerous areas, x-rayed every year, and he would send us a manual of piping that needed to be replaced, especially the ninety-degree elbows coming up to the platform from the pipelines. These sections of pipes had thinned due to erosion.

I guess it was about then that I realized that I had guys' lives in my hands and it began to become very stressful. I began going out at night after work and drinking. I went to nightclubs trying to pick up women. And I'd be out till two or three in the morning and I'd get really horny and I'd pick up prostitutes and get oral sex from them.

My second Section Leader's name was Jeff G.; he was very smart. They selected him to test out the first Subsurface Completion wellhead. I believe that he stayed subsurface in it for two days. It was built by either Boeing or Martin-Marietta. I can't remember which. He was supposed to help them debug it. Unfortunately after they put it in service, one of the maintenance men was in the process of retrieving a pig from the line. A pig is a hard ball about the same outside diameter as the inside diameter of the piping and it's used to unclog the piping from sludge build up in the line. The maintenance man was on the production platform and he hadn't depressurized the line from which the pig would be retrieved. When he opened the chamber to retrieve the pig, it went right through his chest and killed him.

After that Jeff G. had to be transferred; he got kicked upstairs to the business department, so he'd be out of being in close proximity to the offshore people.

Dale G. was a project engineer. His parents had moved to New Orleans to live with him because he had become lonely; so he stayed pretty straight. Dale, was the project engineer for the new Grand Isle 74 facility, which would be included in the Marlin Unit. It would be producing 75,000 cubic feet per day of natural gas. At a wellhead price of $1.00 per cubic foot that would be $75,000 /day. I wrote the shutdown and startup procedures for the central facility that it would be tied into. I also planned on cleaning out a pressure vessel while the platform was shutdown, for the interconnecting piping to be installed. The shutdown and startup procedure had to be approved by my Section Leader, the Production Manager and the Division Operations Manager. The Division Operations Manager's name was Hal R. It turned out that his family had been in the oil business for generations. Hal R. was the only person who had anything to say about the procedures. He wanted one of the flanged pipes on the side of the platform to be flanged closed for safety reasons.

When we shut down the central facility, and had the vessel opened for cleaning. I had them use a venturi to evacuate the vapors from the vessel being cleaned. The flare tower was supposed to have been extinguished, but we didn't realize that just because the flame was no longer at the top of the tower, didn't mean it had been extinguished. Low and behold there was a loud pop at the vessel being cleaned. It startled all of us on the platform. The flame from within the flare tower had traveled down to the pressure vessel we were working on and extinguished itself at the opening in the vessel. A moment of fright, but all was okay.

They seemed to give the really stressful jobs to the young, single people.

There was another guy, named Jay, in the facility engineering department who kept everyone abreast of the latest technology coming out. He had built a project for Bay Marshand, and he built the facility from the ground up. It turned out all the welds were bad and had to be redone. Most of the guys had consultants working with them. Like Brown and Root.

When I got Sick

I'd get back to my apartment about five or six in the morning and then wake up at eight again to get to work by nine again. I did this for about two years. This was very debilitating and I started to feel like a street alcoholic. I could not take care of my apartment any longer and I couldn't hold down my job anymore either.

After I had broken up with Patricia, I was very depressed and I bought a 1978 black Chevy Monte Carlo and instead of purchasing a house for Patricia and myself, I also purchased a house in the ghetto near the French Quarter. The house had like six apartments and I was a slum landlord. It turned out that there were water leaks in the ceilings and that the shingles were all in need of replacement. I contacted the real estate guy that I purchased it from and told him that I wasn't competent when I purchased it and he would have to sell it for me. I had a lawyer and eventually they sold it to a woman from Florida. Later, when I was in the hospital I found out that I was being sued for a million dollars by a guy who tripped going down the stairs because the stairwell banister was loose. He had fallen and broken his neck. Luckily, Joey M. my neighbor was in the insurance business and had told me to get comprehensive insurance coverage and I had. The insurance company investigator found that the man who fell was a trespasser and he had no rights to any insurance money.After I got sick, I first tried a doctor at Tulane. The doctor at Tulane Hospital had said that he could help me; but, when I went back for my next appointment, they told me that he had had a heart attack. I had called my mother and told her what was going on and she said she'd come down. I told her I needed family therapy and she said she would come down and help me. So she flew down and we both flew back to Boston together. I went back to Boston for family therapy. I had a good psychiatrist who recommended that I go to the Newton Wellesley Hospital inpatient unit to see what they could do. It was a state-of-the-art program. When I got there my blood pressure was like 190/110. I was in decrepit condition due to my drinking for about 1½ years and the doctor on call, said that I had to take some Thorazine to be admitted. I didn't want to take it because I thought it could affect my genes. My mother and sister were there with me and I turned to them. My mother said, "You're not coming home with me" and then, I looked at my sister and she said, "You're not coming home with me either, better take it." So it was either the street or take the medication and stay in the inpatient unit. So, I took it.

After a couple of weeks in the inpatient unit at Newton Wellesley, I flew back to New Orleans and tried to resume my life. It still wasn't working out. I was devastated by the loss of Patty. Joey told me that Patty was now going to therapy too.

My psychiatrist in Boston had set me up with a psychiatrist in Louisiana. A Dr. B.; he mostly sat and watched the clock in my sessions. I told him that I had broken the ten commandments by having sex with another man's wife. He responded to me that there were 100 commandments. Then, he would ask me things like how did all the utility poles get constructed across the United States. I had no idea what he was getting at.

We just didn't click. So, I decided that I'd rather leave my job and go back to Massachusetts for better quality treatment.

My mother flew down and I packed up. I had rented a brand-new one-bedroom furnished apartment's worth of furniture from Weiner

Cort Furniture and had, like, only one more payment to make, before I owned it. My mother said to leave it there and not worry about it; so we packed up and I went back to Boston with her in my car., I had sent my books back via Peter Pan or Greyhound Bus Lines.

My Rehabilitation

Once back in Massachusetts, I went between the inpatient psychiatric unit and the outpatient psych unit (the "Day Program") at Newton Wellesley. I really didn't want to live anymore. I was so depressed that I went from the inpatient unit to the outpatient unit on and off for about a year.

Finally, I decided I wanted to live again and try to start over. First, I had to get into a halfway house; it was very difficult. It was hard to get into a halfway house. One of the fellows in the inpatient unit said I could have his spot at the Life Center in Brighton, Massachusetts. So, I stayed there for about three months and I got a job at Goodwill Industries and did contract assembly work. I assembled small items and made like three cents per item, so it's like a dollar an hour. The rehab counselor at Goodwill told me that she had a position for me in the small appliance repair department, if I wanted it; so, I took it. There was just myself and a black guy working there and we were fixing toasters and lamps, that sort of thing.

Then after a couple of weeks, the rehab person told me I could get a job through Temporary Employment Program (TEP) at DBX Industries in Waltham, Massachusetts doing customer service; So, I took that job. My supervisor there, Albeo D. told me that I'd be earning more money if I hadn't come in the way I did, through the TEP program. My TEP person came to visit me a couple of times before she cut me loose.

When I got out of the halfway house, I used an organization called Alternative House and moved into an apartment with two other people: Lisa A. and Mary S. in the Nonantum part of Newton. I made friends with my upstairs neighbors who had parties on the weekends. That's where I first met Sandy W., Joe R., and Bob K. After a couple of months, the owner of the property decided that they were going to turn the property into condominiums. So, Mary, Lisa, and I would have to find alternative living arrangements. The social workers from Alternative Home told us that they had a two-bedroom Section 8 apartment in Wellesley Center. Lisa decided that she wanted to go her own way. But Mary and I decided to take the apartment.

We both cooked one gourmet meal each week for one another. I had my little cubicle next to the shipping room. All I had to do was install a label on the customer returns saying what the customer said was wrong with the unit and place it on a mobile multi-shelf cart. I would get ten or so repairs each day. After placing the label on them, I would bring them to the electronic technician area for repair. The person who did the repairs would return the units to me for cleaning and then, I'd leave them with the packaging department for return to the customer.

When I was finished with the work I had for Customer Service, I volunteered to help out in the shipping department which was right next door to my partitioned area. UPS would come twice a day. Once for pickups and once for drop offs. I learned how to use the UPS. FedEx, and USPS machines for label printout to ship the packages. I learned how to operate a forklift so that when a truck came in with pallets of materials, I could off-load it.

When things were quiet in the shipping room, we'd play around a little bit. Another fellow, Joe, also worked in the shipping area.

One day, the Production Superintendent at DBX came down and said, "I need three guys to take a piece of heavy equipment to Lands-downe Street in Kenmore Square, Boston. He pointed and said you,

you, and you; so I went on the trip with them. We had a two-wheeler and were going up about three or four steps and one of the guys let loose on the three-wheeler and I got a wrenching in my back. By the time I got back to work, I couldn't even sit up straight, my back was hurting so bad. I later learned that I had a herniated disc in my lower back and I'd have to have a spinal tap if I wanted to prove it. Then, I could have collected workman's compensation. I had found out that you could die when they did a spinal tap and I didn't feel it was necessary that I work in that department anymore.

After the shipping room accident, I was on the floor in the living room a lot. Mary got fed up with me because I was blocking the living room. Mary went back to Middlesex Community College and took a review course in nursing and she got a job at Brigham and Women's Hospital as a nurse in the Infectious Disease Department. She was a bit of a control freak; while she was there, she was having power struggles with her boss and finally she got her boss's job. She told me that the rent that she had to pay for the Section 8 apartment was higher than if she went to the free market. So she was going to get another apartment and she asked me if I wanted to go with her. I wasn't ready to move yet. I wasn't in love with Mary. We were just friends, so I didn't want to move in with her. Plus my back was still bad, I was reading every book I could find on lower backs with disc injuries. Most of the books told what exercises to do. The only book that was good was Maggie Letvack's book on lower backs. She didn't recommend any exercises.

I put a 4'x8' piece of plywood on my bed. I slept on that for a year and slowly got into the fetal position by stretching my muscles a little more each day, and I added pillows under my legs and hip. I had to keep my spine parallel to the piece of plywood, then slowly the sciatica subsided and I was doing better. By then, the social workers got me a new roommate, Lou Z. He ended up being a useless bastard. He didn't want to work, just hang out all the time. He wasn't contributing to the apartment. So I had it out with him and he moved on. The social workers said that they had two new tenants they wanted to bring in who had been institutionalized. They wanted to experiment with people to see if they could function in the real world after they'd had long-term institutionalization.

They didn't leave me homeless, however. They said they had a private apartment for me in Newton Upper Falls with two other guys. Sandy W. and Bob C. were going to be my new roommates. Sandy W. worked at DBX in the wood room matching two wooden panels together for each unit. Bob had been working at some electronics company in Watertown, but shortly after I moved in, he took a job as a taxi driver.

Sandy studied proverbs and whenever he spoke, words of wisdom would come out. He bought an encyclopedia with a lot of color pictures in it that he studied. He smoked non-filtered Camel cigarettes.

I loved Sandy like the brother that I never had. Sandy was a descendent from the Winslows who had come over on the Mayflower. His aunt in England sent him a scratch art kit as a gift and he was up and running. He loved art. He made his own frames out of wood and would hand his art out or sell it to anyone. I think that he had done oil painting before the scratch art. He loved the scratch art, though. He could do his free associations on the scratch board along with drawings. His artwork looked a little like Aztec artwork. Sandy's favorite saying was "I'm dead!" We used to say it together and laugh. I used to sing some songs with him that he had taught me.

One of our favorites was "Southern Man" by Neil Young.

I have one of his scratch art pieces in my storage unit that I picked up off the street. It's just kind of weird stuff. The writing on the art piece is whatever came to him from his free association. He taught me how to play one song on the recorder: "Three Blind Mice."

He asked me if I wanted to go to Second Story with him, which was like a club that you could go to after work on Friday nights and have dinner and play some ping-pong. We had a great time. Back then, if you cooked the meal, you could have a free meal. The director when I went there was a woman named Eileen. She taught me how to cook in a wok. There was a girl named Beth W., one of the counselors, and a guy named Don H., also a counselor. I used to go out to Harvard Square in Cambridge on Saturday night to try and pick up women with Steve A. We saw Don H. driving a taxi in Harvard Square. Rivkah, an Israeli gal, had become the director after Eileen and she once told me to be careful what I said because the walls have ears.

Sandy was a very talented person. He could play almost any instrument. I think that he liked playing his electronic keyboard the most, though. He had cut an album with Barry from Jordan's Furniture when he was in high school. The title of the album was *The Art of Lovin*. Sandy played the drums in that band. Sandy could play the violin, the flute, and the guitar. He took a bus down to New York to purchase a Sitar, and when he brought it home, he hooked up regular guitar strings to it and a pickup so he could play it through an amplifier. He was truly amazing.

I asked my boss at DBX for a job in the electromechanical assembly department and they gave me a job doing repairs. The technicians would identify which components needed to be replaced and I would do the replacements, replace the housing on the units and give them back to the new customer service guy for return to the customer.

Well, there was a guy there that I worked next to whose name was Raul V. He sat next to me at his workbench and was the supervisor for the electromechanical department. He was going on vacation and he asked me to sit in for him while he was away. It turned out that one or two of the guys were stealing units. One of the guys was caught taking a unit into the bathroom, dropping it down with a rope to another guy at the bottom, next to the building. At about 3:00 p.m. they would do "Besurah" (trash); the fellas would each take their trash buckets with them and bring them down the stairs and empty them into the dumpster. Evidently, the management found out that somebody had been dumping units in there and then retrieving them after work so the Production Superintendent told me that I would have to check the buckets before they went down the stairs to the dumpster. I didn't want to search around in their trash because that wasn't my job.

So I delegated the responsibility of going through the trash baskets to the fella who was sitting at the end. He went and complained to the vice president that he was new there and shouldn't have that kind of responsibility, so the production superintendent came out and told me that I was on shaky ground, that he had told me to do it and not somebody else.

The other thing that I did when I sat in for Raul was ask the people working in the department what could be done to make them happier. They all started yelling "more money, more money." I guess I was kind of rocking the boat a little, because I believe the vice president, Jim P. heard. His office was right off the Electromechanical Assembly Department area.

I decided that the problem they were having was getting all the parts for the units. They only had enough parts to make ¾ of a unit. Then, they would put that unit on a shelf under their bench and start on another unit. So, I met with the production planner and asked him for a list of units they need for the next month or so and then went to the parts department and gave them a list of components we needed for the next month to try and plan ahead. The Parts Department basically blew me off and I heard Jim P. tell the parts guy, "Good job."

I waited about a week or two and on a Friday afternoon when I couldn't stand it anymore, I said to myself, *I'm not working here anymore.* I walked out and went to the Unemployment Division in Newton Corner and said that I had just got laid off from my job and I needed to collect. The woman said wait a minute, I have to go check something and she came back a few minutes later and told me that she had spoken to the production superintendent and that I had left voluntarily, so that I didn't get fired and couldn't collect.

So, there I was out in the street without a job; no income coming in and went back to my apartment and I was starting to get suicidal again and my folks decided that I needed to go to the hospital again. The doctor that I had before, told me there were no openings in Newton- Wellesley and that I would have to go to Bournewood Hospital, in Brookline, Massachusetts. I had decided it was a middle-of-the-road decision whether I needed to go or not. I got out of the car in the middle of the road about ¼ of the way there. My father got out of his car and came to meet me. I think that I told him that I wasn't going and tried to hit him, but he hit me first and then my mother called an ambulance or the police. I can't remember which.

When I got there they told me I'd have to come in and do some paperwork upstairs. so I went upstairs in this building and went to sign some paperwork. Afterwards, I discovered that I was in a locked door unit. I stayed there for a couple of weeks. There wasn't even wallpaper on the walls, it was a dump. Quite a few of the other patients were getting Electroconvulsive Therapy (ECT). Mary S. and Sandy W. friends of mine, had had ECT for depression and both had memory loss due to ECT. I didn't want to have it. They were giving it to people right and left, so I decided that maybe if I tried to help serve lunch and stuff like that, clean up after the patients ate, it would help me get out of there. They let us go to Occupational Therapy, which was in another building next door. I decided I would try and escape. I took off and I walked all the way to my family's house about four miles away. I didn't have a key, so I went in through the basement window. When my parents came home, they were all pissed off and they told me I had to go back to Bournewood. I went back, tried to escape one more time, and one of the workers and I were out in the street and I tried to push him into an oncoming car, but he got me in like a three-point hold and took me back. Later, that same guy was very nice to me and he had made a special relationship with me. He said, "I hear you got into some deep s*** down in New Orleans." Then he said, "You've got to forget about it." After a couple of weeks, I was so excited when they let me go into the open house on the campus.

After I got transferred to the open house on the campus, I took a walk on the grounds and I was really angry; there was a dog on the grounds and I took a big rock and tried to throw it at the dog to kill it. But it kept moving and I couldn't hit it. So, I finally gave up.

Everybody in the house was suicidal and homicidal. It scared the hell out of me, so I figured I better get a job. I got the *Boston Globe* and found a job at a dry cleaners in Belmont, Massachusetts. After the first interview, they told me that they had hired someone else, but would keep me in mind if things didn't work out. About two or three days later, they called me back and said the person they hired wasn't doing very well and that he had left the job, so it was available to me if I wanted it. I took the job. It was a pretty easy job. I had to press, iron, and steam clothes to make them neat and they also made me a front-end clerk. I helped the customers at the front counter by bringing in clothes that needed to be processed and retrieving clothes that the customers were picking up. Plus, I collected the money and operated the register. The people who owned the store were a black family. The father and son, Bill and Paul P. mostly ran the place, plus the mother, Alice, came in to help part time a couple of days per week. They were really very refined people. The son had gone out to California after finishing school, but I guess it hadn't worked out well, so he came back to Massachusetts broke and ended up working with his father at the shop. There was another woman who worked there—Ginny; she put tags on the clothes, bagged them and placed them on the rack in alphabetical order. There was also a guy Ben who was spotting and operating the cleaning equipment in the back and then a fellow, Joe B. working next to me at another press. He only steamed and pressed clothes. He was a real survivor. He was quite the guy.

They treated me like I've never been treated on a job before. The father would buy lunch every day or almost every day and I got a nice Christmas bonus every year. I had to sit in one time for the family, when the family's parents had passed away in North Carolina. They'd be away Saturday and then come back on Monday. But like I said I was there for about six years and I developed a lot of anxiety. I started having panic attacks. I thought I was going to drop dead on the job. My doctor Penny A. gave me Valium to deal with it. She diagnosed me with Chronic Anxiety. One day, the panic attacks were so bad I just walked out of the store and didn't look back.

Well, after working at the cleaners, I went to TAC (Temporary Accounting and Clerical) Corp. and they got me a temporary job in a company called Shipley in Wellesley. It was some kind of a chemical manufacturing company, but I couldn't figure out what chemical(s) they produced. I was just folding brochures and making plates for the four-color printing press, which Ken T. ran. Ken was a cool guy that worked there, but the job was very unstable because they didn't know whether they could hire me permanently. Business wasn't that good. A couple of college kids came through to help out. They left and said they were going to do landscaping. So eventually, I decided I'd go do landscaping too. I had a couple of credit cards and a little money in the bank, so I started my own company called Garden City Landscaping.

The landlord where I was living for six years with Sandy and Bob didn't want me to store my equipment in the basement, so I moved. Bob's love of his life came to live with him in the house with her two or three kids and it just wasn't working out. I told Bob it wasn't right that he had to find a place for himself and his girlfriend and his girlfriend's kids. so he finally did. We had this one potential roommate come in to look over the apartment. He had been a neurologist and something bad had happened when he did some brain surgery, so he switched over to becoming a urologist and he and his wife weren't getting along, so he separated from his wife. He was living in the apartment with us and he didn't know how to do anything for himself.

He would just sit and watch TV in his room all day and at night go do his shift at the hospital. He was an Egyptian guy, and one day we were looking out the front door and he said to me, "Is that really what you want to do?" And then I said, "Yeah." Then he said, "You know I'm supposed to kill you because I say salaam alaichum and you say shalom aleichem." I responded to him, "Yeah, isn't that stupid?" About a couple of months later, he decided to move back in with his wife because I don't think he knew how to cook for himself. His wife had been doing everything for him and I guess he realized it after separating from her for a while. I said something like, "You know when you make a commitment you should stick with it," when he left the apartment prematurely.

We got this other guy in for an interview for the open bedroom. His name was Vito. He was from Pennsylvania. He got a job as an accountant for the Commonwealth of Massachusetts and he was Sicilian; he was a real bastard. The first thing he did when we showed him the apartment was keep the key to the room. I was going to move to the front room and he was going to take the backroom so when he came back and said he wanted the room, I thought it was funny because he was a crooked thief. He told me a story about when he was in the Air Force, he had left a screwdriver in one of the engine compartments and it caused a plane to go down. So, anyways to make a long story short, he tortured Sandy; he knew I wouldn't take it from him. He used to bring his friends and they played cards downstairs in the living room.

Well, the landlord and I didn't get along about the equipment in the basement, so I went to visit another place in Nonantum, another village in Newton. There were about seven housemates in the house. I would have a roof over my head. The landlord, who just happened to be a Jewish guy, didn't mind if I stored my equipment in the basement or on the grounds.

There was an older guy, Steve, and he was kind of cool, a lawyer named Anthony N., who was a black guy and there were a few other housemates. When I went in for an interview to meet everybody, there was one guy that I couldn't meet, supposedly he was on vacation.

Eventually that fellow came back and it turned out that he'd been in jail and he had a gun in the house. Anthony would get drunk almost every night and beat up his girlfriend, Eileen who was living there too. Their room was above mine and I had to buy ear plugs so I could sleep at night.

It turned out that they weren't paying the bills (electric and gas). They'd go to court and tell them that they didn't have the money to pay the bills and the court would give them a continuance. Finally, I told them that they would have to pay the bills or leave and they weren't happy about that at all. I put a lock on my bedroom door and they broke down the door and came into my room. I just stood there and let them do whatever they wanted to. They just came over to me and pushed me and I fell back on the bed and lay there.

A friend of mine, Kevin W., was living in a rooming house in Newton Corner (another village in Newton); he told me there was an opening for me if I wanted to move there. It was a furnished room; so, I met with the landlord and I moved in. There was one bed, a little room with a shower and a toaster oven in it. so it was kind of peaceful and quiet and it was just what I needed for a fresh new start.

I told the guys at the house on California Street in Nonantum the next day that I was out of there. The day I left, two other housemates left with me. They didn't like what was going on there either it turned out.

I did landscaping for two years. The first year we did a lot of landscape architecture, construction, and maintenance. We did a lot of new installations. We did everything from laying sod, seeding a new lawn, planting tulips, planting flower beds. We installed new pyramidal arborvitae bushes and yews. We did everything the first year. When I was pricing the job I would just list the costs for materials, labor, and equipment. I didn't know that you were supposed to double that for overhead. So, by the second year I didn't have any money left. I'd been paying out of my credit cards. So in the second year I just did gardening by myself. Plus, I had $10,000 in credit card debt. I tried to get a business loan to keep the business going, but they said that I had to be in business for at least four years before I could get a business loan.

I ended up in the hospital one way or another and there was a patient there who was a lawyer, and he told me that if I was just paying the interest and not able to pay any of the principal, I might as well go bankrupt; it'd be cheaper for me and in about three years I'd have my credit back.

He also told me that I could keep my car as long as I kept making the payments on it.

So, I did that when I got out of the hospital. I hired a lawyer, Atty. Donald B. and for about $4000.00, he processed a bankruptcy for me. I met with an administrative judge and I explained what had transpired and he said, "Don't ever do that again" and discharged my credit card debt.

So, I ended up in a rooming house. It was relatively safe. Kevin was a good friend of mine and later it turned out he was dating another friend of mine, Barbara C. who I was also close with.

I went to a company called Sullivan & Cogliano, an employment agency. I told them that I had three years of engineering school. It was hard to get a job if they thought that you were overqualified. They got me a couple of temporary jobs such as installing components on circuit boards. Then they got me a job at Candela laser in Natick. Candela had two buildings right next to each other. One was the manufacturing building and the other building was the R&D Department. I was in the manufacturing building constructing lasers, power supplies, distribution boxes, and heat exchangers. I built about $5 million worth of lasers in one year. The number of employees went from about 40 to 100. The production superintendent, Dick H., told Sullivan & Cogliano to send him five more like me. He bought out my contract from Sullivan and Cogliano and I was given permanent employee status.

They got an industrial building in Wayland and brought both buildings under one roof.

A purchasing agent knew a friend of mine from college, Jim Snyder, and I guess he had talked to Jim about me and Jim had told him that I had a master's degree. Someone once said to me they didn't like it when you lied, so anyways I was there for about three years and I went from the analog type laser department in which we built a lot of R&D lasers for universities, etc. to the solid-state urology lasers section.

The Urological Lithotriptor would function as follows:

A fiber optic cable with a camera and a basket were inserted through the urethra into the kidney and then once the kidney stone was in the basket they would blast it with a laser beam. It would fragment and then the basket of fragmented stone would be pulled out via the urethra.

I became like the supervisor of the department unofficially and I was going from the R&D Department to the Manufacturing Department to bring the prototype into mass production. The owner of the company, the CEO, Horace F. wanted one unit out the door per week. They cost $150,000 each. But there were bugs in the units. They hadn't been debugged yet and I knew something was going wrong in the Quality Control Department. They were supposed to test them for proper operation before they were released for shipment. They were letting units go out the door that weren't operating properly. I had a sense of what was going on.

In the meantime, I had enrolled in electronics courses at Lowell Tech at MIT and had an electronics instructor, Mr. B., who could preach electronics. He was in love with electronics and I learned a lot from him. I learned how to analyze almost any analog circuit. When I went to take the digital electronics classes after the two analog courses, I was working in the lab during the day at my job, building and testing power supplies—which produced ten joules of energy. I told the instructor at the electronics class that every new Urology Lithotriptor that was being built was a revised version and he said that it didn't sound good and that I should leave there.

So, to make a long story short. I wasn't feeling well. I thought that I was going to drop dead because the building was about a football field in length and I was walking back and forth all day from the R&D Department to the Manufacturing Department, transitioning the prototype to mass production.

There was a new employee at the bench behind me who was from Texas. I trained him to build the power supplies and he kept screwing them up and he said, "I'm just here kicking ass and taking names." Wise guy from Texas and everything he was building was f***** up. So, anyway I had to repair all those that he screwed up. Plus, some other wiseass guy who came from another laser company that had gone out of business, Chuck J., had started testing my power supplies and transformers. He started destructive testing of the power supplies and transformers. I wasn't happy. I'd build something and he'd destroy it in his study. I got frustrated with that and complained to my boss. My boss told me that there was nothing he could do, since he wasn't Chuck's boss.

There was another guy in the Medical Laser Department named Ray. Horace called all the people working on the urology lasers into his office. He said that he was being embarrassed, that all these hospitals were calling and saying that the Urological Lithotripters weren't operating properly. Ray told Horace, the CEO, that he'd take care of the problem with the units. So, they made him supervisor of the section. I wasn't going to take it on. I wanted to duck out.

Eventually, they hired an electrical engineer and paid him a thousand bucks an hour to debug the unit. There was a lot of arcing taking place inside the unit (unintentional grounding; I believe—I think that he was trying to shield everything.) I don't think that he was able to do it, though. I left before I could find out.

So my psychiatrist told me I was suffering from depression, when I was having panic attacks and thought I was going to drop dead on the shop floor.

Steve D., who had trained me on the power supplies said to me if you're suffering from depression, it's not worth it. Poor Steve had gotten shoulder cancer, had some sort of treatments for it, but he later passed away from it.

Dick H., the founder who hired me, had some serious illness and he also passed away while I was there.

My psychiatrist prescribed an antidepressant for me known as Wellbutrin. Two days after I started taking it, I went into the Human Resource Department and gave my two weeks' notice. The machine shop foreman, Kevin P., said to me, "All you're doing is turning your other cheek." He said, "I'm leaving on Friday with no notice."

When my boss, the production supervisor, John S. found out that I was leaving, he came over to me and said, "Is it money you need, Larry?" So, I said, "No, it wasn't." I had started working on a dermatology laser and I didn't want to die over something cosmetic.

So from Candela Laser, I found a job doing telemarketing for $18 an hour at a company called General Development. It was like a laser, the way that floor would turn on and the whole place would brighten up when people were on the phones. I thought that I'd eventually go into real estate and use my Real Estate Broker's license.

I got contacted by Jerry G. to see if I wanted to do some engineering work in the factory that he had inherited from his father. The factory was located in Brockton, Massachusetts, about a forty-minute drive each way to and from where I lived.

I've Been Rehabilitated

Jerry asked me how many digits I was earning, and I told him five. He asked me what I was currently earning and said that he would match it. Well, this was my chance to get back into engineering after twelve years away from it. I retained state-of-the-art technical expertise from my job at Candela three years earlier. Jerry was interested in possibly using a laser to make seals on plastic bags. His business mostly made converting machinery attachments for the plastic industry such as oval handle cutouts, hole punchers for things such as grape bags and display items, reinforced cutouts for handle bags, bottom sealing equipment for inline separation of plastic-bag serrators, and handle cutouts for banana bags, etc.

I thought about it and I said okay, but I asked Jerry what I could do after I got burned out from designing machinery and he said that I could do inside sales. So, I went to work at his company, working out back of the manufacturing office. Jerry had given me a drawing board and the inhouse carpenter, Fred, built an office around me while I was working on my first machine. They had assigned me to design a shuttle for a handle cutout. There was a company up in New Hampshire that had a bag machine that I would be designing the attachment for. I think I completed the design in three weeks and there was a lot of pressure on me. All the employees seemed very unhappy that a friend of Jerry's had been brought in. So, I knew that I had to get this machine right.

Jerry was bringing some of our friends from high school over for lunch one day and he asked me if I wanted to go out with them and I said no. In three weeks, I had the first machine designed and it fit on the other bag machine that it was attached to, just as if it was made for it, which it was. I had gone out to the company and taken some measurements to make sure it would fit properly. When Ted A., the field service guy, went out to install it, he put a "Made in the USA" sign on it. It worked so beautifully and made handle cutouts on a bag machine that wasn't designed for it. I don't know how much he charged for the shuttle, but I thought that he made a mistake in not selling them to Battenfeld Gloucester, the main bag machine manufacturer who could install them during manufacture of the bag machine.

Jerry had told me that some MIT guys said that it couldn't be done. Well, I had done it. I used a piece of string and some pins to determine the length of the drive belt. There was a nip roller to adjust where the handle would be cut out and since the attachment was made for a continuous bag machine, it had to take the plastic off the machine and process it through the attachment, which had a few handle cutout machines across the bank.

Well, I was at Jerry's plant for about six years. Steve L., the VP of Marketing, was kind of my boss. He would come in and give me new ideas for machines and I came up with a couple of my own. I was designing about three or four new products per year. I got a patent on a zipper attachment machine that I had done the engineering and design on. Jerry paid me $1.00 for the patent.

While I was working at Jerry's, I met a Jewish woman at a ballroom dance, Caron C. She told me that she had been separated from her husband for like six months. After our first date, she told me she had a baby, less than a year old. So, I got to experience what it was like to take care of a baby. One night I was at Caron's apartment and the baby climbed out of the crib and landed on her feet. Caron was overwhelmed with the baby landing on her feet and I said, "Caron, this is very dangerous. We should put a tent up over the crib so she can't do it again." So, I bought a tent and installed it over the crib. She gave me oral sex the first time I went to bed with her. She said to me, "I know what you want," unzipped my pants and gave me oral sex, then I fornicated with her. She was the best oral sex that I ever had.

I was living in the rooming house and I hadn't shown her where I lived because I felt embarrassed. She wanted to see where I lived, so I took her to my house and she told me that a cousin of hers had lived in a place like that. We had sex in the bed. She was on top of me and I rotated around to give her cunnilingus while she was giving me oral sex. I licked her vagina once and didn't like doing it because of her pubic hair. She said, "Lick me" and I wouldn't. I didn't feel comfortable doing it. She said, "You licked me once. Lick me again." I didn't do it again, though.

I was head over heels in love with her. The sex was great and she was very smart. She was a Columbia graduate and had a master's degree in audiology. She worked at the Fernald School in Waltham, Massachusetts. Later one day, she told me that she was going out skiing on the weekend with a guy from work. I sensed that Caron was playing around with (an/other guy(s) and having sex with him/them.

I left her at her door after a date and we had a shouting contest through the window at night. I told her that I was in love with her and she said that I was just obsessed with her. She told me that she couldn't afford to do that in case her husband had some private investigators making sure her life was stable and that she could take care of the baby.

The day came for her divorce in court and it turned out to be a real big snowstorm. I told her that I'd go with her, but she didn't want me in the courtroom because it might be grounds for her to lose custody of her daughter, another boyfriend; so, she went by herself. Finally, she told me that she thought she was a nymphomaniac and so, I stopped chasing after her. I remember one day, right after I had stopped seeing her we had a big snowstorm. I went over and I shoveled out her car. I felt bad for her.

So, I had had the experience of having a baby and I wanted to have a child.

After working two years at Jerry's, I met another Jewish woman at a United Jewish Singles Dance. I ran into Lou Z. there, who had shared the apartment in Wellesley with me for a short time and while we were talking, he noticed this gal coming by and he said that he knew her and he introduced me to her. That was when I met Janice A., my now ex-wife. We dated and liked the same things: movies, plays, musicals, and going out to dinner. Her apartment was well decorated with all the necessary props. She lived in Cambridge near Harvard Square in a one-bedroom apartment. The building had rent control and she had lived there quite a while. I knew that she came from a relatively wealthy family. In fact her sister Diane, had been the first female VP at TIAA Cref. She had made several million dollars while working there.

I was dating Janice; she was forty-one years old. We both wanted to have a child. I had told her that I was taking an antidepressant. I was also on an antipsychotic medication, which I didn't tell her about; I told her that I wanted to adopt a child. She said that she had worked as a social worker when she was younger, and that all the children up for adoption had problems. I spoke with Dr. A., my psychiatrist, and asked her whether the meds that I was taking could affect childbirth. She said, "No, it was too toxic." I called my neurologist and the receptionist there told me that a lot of men called to see if the meds that they're taking could affect childbirth and she said, "No, they couldn't."

So, I decided to go ahead with having our own child. I knew that Janice was pretty well off financially if anything should happen. I was, however, leery of the fact that the medications only warn women who are anticipating childbirth to consult with their doctors before taking them.

I had been designing machinery for six years. I wasn't much of a salesman at that time. I didn't really want to be in sales and went to a couple of trade shows in Chicago with Jerry, Steve, and Teddy.

The second time that I went to the trade show in Chicago, I was so full of anxiety, I thought I was going to drop dead, so I ended up in the bathroom hiding in one of the stalls trying to calm myself down from the panic attacks I was having. Finally, the day was over and I went back to the hotel.

I mentioned it to everyone I knew—that men provide about ½ the DNA for the child and so, what they're taking should affect the childbirth.

I got her pregnant and we were going to have the baby, but I think she killed the baby by going overboard physically. After a couple of months, she had a miscarriage and the fetus died in the womb. I think that she killed it by working herself to death. I don't think that she wanted to have a child out of wedlock.

A fellow that I worked with Steve L., the aforementioned VP at Park Air, told me that he and his wife had had a miscarriage and waited seven years before trying again. He recommended that we not wait, that we should try again immediately. He had regretted waiting so long.

I proposed to Janice on my knee at Good Harbor Beach in 1992. She said, "Let me think about it," and a few minutes later said, "Okay."

Well, Janice and I were married at the Sail Loft in Cambridge in November of 1992. It was a nice restaurant and we had rented it out for the day. I had arranged to have Rabbi A. perform the ceremony. We had a chuppah and he made us a beautiful Jewish wedding certificate and made a special service for us. I was very anxious, panicky, but I looked at Diane, Janice's sister and she gave me the strength to continue on. We exchanged wedding bands. I believe that I had Adam, my nephew, as the best man.

In my sixth year at Park Air, Jerry went outside our vertical market and got a contract to install a metallic reflective sleeve over a nylon woven sleeve for Land Rovers from a company called Bently Harris in Exton, Pennsylvania. They were putting on the metallic sleeve manually and they wanted to automate it. They had specifications for the metallic sleeve. I believe that there were about three or four different diameters and lengths and they wanted the metallic sheath to be heat sealed to the nylon sleeve. The finished product would be installed over rubber hose in the Rover's engine compartment, thereby reflecting the heat from the engine, thus allowing them to make the engine compartment smaller.

I did the cost estimate for the machine, and gave it to Jerry, he doubled it and got the contract to build the machine. I believe that he was charging $150,000 for the machine. It was going to be a year-long project. Everything almost went fine. A salesman talked me into using an indexing drive motor, which was a bit of a mistake, but it worked okay. Then, I couldn't get a good knife for the guillotine that would cut the sleeves to the desired length. The blades would wear out rather quickly while cutting through the foil and nylon sleeve. Finally, I couldn't get the extruder to work well. I only had two or three weeks to design it and get it to work. I could get it to work okay, but it wasn't easy. Jerry came down and wanted to see the machine work. He said something to the effect that it never worked, did it? I guess that he had heard that it wasn't working. It had an interface panel that you could input the length of sleeve that you wanted and I had designed a spiral roll windup that went from one side of the reel to the other.

I set up the extruder, turned the machine on and got it to work for Jerry. He told them to ship it to the customer. The customer was calling me weekly for updates. They were in a hurry to get the machine. I just didn't have the time to get the extruder to work easier.

I made a trip to Bentley Harris after they had received the machine, evidently, it was tripping the circuit breaker. There was an engineer there that had told me that he had just finished up a new train or trolley project in Canada. When I got there, I had read the entire manual on the motor for the machine and on page one or two, it had said that you could decrease the current drawn by doing something in the settings on the motor controller panel. So, the other engineer mentioned it to me and I said, "Yes, that should work." So, we did that and it prevented it from tripping the breaker. We were discussing the extruder section of the machine and I noticed some of the components from the extruder were missing. There was a black woman who was operating the machine. I told her that I just had a son. That he was about two years old now and she seemed happy about that. She told me that she was able to get the machine to work okay.

They had one big room in which the nylon was being automatically woven into a sleeve. It looked like something from another planet.

Keith's Birth

In Sept.1993, my son Keith was born. I made myself into an obstetrician by studying books on obstetrics. I didn't want a second miscarriage. He had gone breach after a couple of months of pregnancy. A friend of my, then wife Janice had had the baby manipulated in the womb so that it would come out feet first; however, the baby had impinged on the umbilical court and she had a stillbirth. The doctor that did the manipulation was going to get sued for millions. Janice had had an amniocentesis to make sure the baby didn't have Down Syndrome. After that, Janice and I just rode it out and when it was about time for birth. We scheduled a planned C-section. The pregnancy was pretty typical. Janice allowed herself to have one cup of wine the whole nine months of pregnancy. The Beth Israel Obstetrician had Janice going in every couple of days towards the end for an ultrasound. I think all that stress caused Janice to go into labor the night before the planned C-section. An older guy at work had said to me, "You're not going to get any sleep tonight" when I left work. I just shrugged him off. I knew that the C-Section wasn't scheduled until about 7:00 a.m. the next morning. We had done a dry run of the quickest route to Beth Israel Hospital, so we were ready. We had met with the Obstetrician who was going to perform the C-Section and we had met with the anesthesiologist to plan what kind of anesthesia he'd be giving her.

When I got home that night I went to sleep about 10:00 p.m. I got woken up about 11:00 p.m. when Janice said, "Larry, my water broke." Her friend had told her to take a shower after water breaks before she goes in for the surgery because there's a lot of sweat and perspiration. She went in for the shower and I waited outside the bathroom to listen to her.

All of a sudden she said to me, "I'm starting to have contractions." I started to measure the time in between the contractions and they started getting closer and closer, so, I said, "Okay I'm going to call the hospital and tell them that you're having contractions and to get ready for your C-section." By then, it was about 12:00 p.m. to 1:00 a.m. So, I drove her to the hospital, got out of the car and got her a wheelchair. I wheeled her up to the delivery room and they hooked her up to a machine that monitored the contractions like a ticker tape. They told us that the doctor who had planned to do the C-section wasn't available, but there was a female physician available who could do it. Also, an anesthesiologist came by and told us what anesthesia he was going to use. It was different than the one that was planned, and so I had a disagreement with him. Finally, the doctor came in and told the anesthesiologist that the one that was pre-planned would be fine.

I was planning on being in the operating room for her and the baby and I told the staff to only bring me in once, I wouldn't see any blood and guts. So, they told me that they'd situate me above her neck, so that I would be able to see her face and head. When they called me into the operating room, they brought me in from her feet first, so I saw her whole guts hanging out. But, I went quickly past and they had set up a barrier between her neck and head. I sat down in a chair that they gave me at her head and Janice said to me, "Can you scratch my nose, it's itchy." I said, "sure" if that was all that was bothering her, I'd gladly oblige her. Then the anesthesiologist came by and said that he could tweak the medication that she was getting to get rid of the itchy nose. So, we agreed.

So when the baby came out it was all black and I said, must have been a recessive gene. I said I don't care. I'll love him anyway black or white. So then, they washed the blood off him and he was white. The baby did a 9 on the test that they give to all new infants.

When Keith came out with five fingers and five toes on each side, I thought okay, it's going to be okay. I thought he'd be fine. Janice was taken to the recovery room and I was exhausted. My family had come up to the hospital and it was about four or five in the morning I was totally wiped out and was having a lot of anxiety attacks, so I went home to get a couple of hours of sleep.

My sister and my mother and my father stayed with Janice in the hospital and I went back about seven or so, after staying home a couple of hours. I told them that we wanted him to get circumcised by a medical doctor, not by a mohel, because my nephew had a mohel do it and it had to be redone. So, I had a little circumcision ceremony and prayer.

Janice was in the hospital for two days. That's all the insurance company allotted back then. They allowed her two days and the La Leche League of women (Nazis of breastfeeding) got her to link up and breastfeed Keith, almost immediately. I never thought it would happen because Janice is such a wimp. When she started breastfeeding okay, they let us out.

We stopped along the Charles River on Greenough Boulevard, in Watertown on the way home; it was a rather warm day, and we welcomed our new baby into the world with all its beauty.

We took him home that day. We had a helper at home, Susan M. to take care of her while she was at home with the baby for about two to three weeks healing up from the C-section. I was going to work. She stayed home for three months with the baby, nursing him and then she went back to work. We hired this woman that had been trained and worked for two doctors to take care of him while we were at work and about a month or two into that she had become pregnant herself and she decided to move to Florida where the welfare laws were better for her. So, we lost our nanny. Then we hired another nanny while we were living on Centre Street, in Newton Corner and she turned out to be dishonest. She told us that somebody was trying to break into the apartment one day.

We were planning on going to Florida to see my folks who stayed there during the winter months and we changed the door locks, because we didn't want her to have a key to get in there and steal anything. When we got back, Keith was going into a nursery at about six months of age. All of a sudden he stopped sleeping at night. He was up all night and Janice and I were both working full-time so we couldn't function at work, if we were up all night with him. My sister told me to go into the nursery and make believe I was a fly on the wall and see what was going on. I observed that all they were doing was rocking him to sleep all day and putting him in the crib and having him sleep so they didn't have to take care of him. I told Janice, this is not good, let's get him out of there.

When Keith turned one, we bought a house. We didn't want him on a main street. It was too dangerous. We hired another nanny. Jennifer and after about two or three months I got the phone bill. She must have been calling all over the United States during the day; probably, on the phone five to six hours a day and Keith was being neglected.

We got Keith into a preschool in Newton Highlands (another village of Newton) in a church basement. The Director of the preschool said that Keith needed an aide for himself. Jennifer went in as his aid and then reported back that he didn't need an aid. so, I had to fire her. She had told us that the person that she gave us as a reference would tell us not to hire her, but Jennifer said that the only reason the person would say that was because she wanted her back to work for her.

So, I went in and acted as his aide.

I'd act as a magnet for the other kids to play with him. I'd set up blocks to make a museum. We put some dinosaurs in it.

By then, Keith had had about 100 expressive words and he started losing words at around twenty months of age. I was getting scared, so we took him to his pediatrician and she said that some children lose words and then they have a sudden surge and make a lot of progress later. Anyways, he kept losing words and I went into the Pediatrician's office and started screaming at her that there was something wrong. She said bring him to a speech pathologist to see what was going on; Janice took him to the Speech Pathologist. I was working. Before the speech pathologist would see him, in the same office, he had to see an audiologist in the other office. The audiologist took one look at him and Janice said she got pale white and then, she went to the speech pathologist office later on.

When Janice got home, she received a call from Keith's Pediatrician recommending that he be seen by a team of specialists. There was something seriously wrong with his development.

Janice was shocked that the Pediatrician told her this over the phone without having us go into her office to be told and discuss it.

Keith's Diagnosis and Treatment

Later on we found out via a telephone call from the doctor that he had PDD NOS (Pervasive Developmental Disorder Not Otherwise Specified). We had to take him to a team of specialists at Boston Children's Hospital. A woman with an MS in Education, a PhD Speech Pathologist, and an Occupational Therapist. It was awful, just awful. The Speech Pathologist said that he would be able to speak but it's going to be really, really hard. Then said that he had to go into early intervention.

We hooked up with a pediatric neurologist. Dr. R. at Boston's floating Hospital. He was the Chief of the Department and wanted us to do a twenty-four-hour EEG on Keith. For some reason every doctor that we went to wanted to measure his head. I finally told Janice that if one more doctor did that, I was going to kill them.

Well, Dr. R. explained to us what was happening. Evidently, a child develops neurotypically the first year and then in the second year of development, the Autism neurology begins to develop in the brain. So, it was like a battle. While the brain had its plasticity, we would have to try and stave off the Autism neurology by intense therapy and if we could neutralize the Autism progression, he could become fairly normal. He recommended doing a lot of play with him and the ABA (Applied Behavior Analysis) program.

We also had a local Neurologist, named Dr. S., who said that there had been this tiny study with some children and they were given some Amantadine, typically used as an antiviral, but it had improved their condition according to Dr. S.

I told Janice that I was against Keith taking it, but she wanted to go along with the doctor.

So, Keith took the Amantadine for a few years.

When Keith was about fifteen years old, I was called to the Charles Brown Middle school, where he was attending. The nurse said that Keith wasn't feeling well and I needed to pick him up. So. I was at the school in ten minutes. I went to the nurse's office. He looked a little pale and so I said that I'd take him home. I was parked across the lane at the front of the building and when we were walking across the lane. Keith started to collapse. I grabbed him before he could fall and held on to him. There was some construction work going on at the school. They had a fire truck there. One of the firemen came over to me and asked whether I wanted help to get Keith into the car. I answered, "Yes, please." We put Keith in the passenger right front seat and he looked as if he was going to turn blue. So, I asked the firemen if he could call an ambulance and he said sure right away.

Well, the ambulance got there in like seven minutes and they put Keith in the back and the EMT asked me if I wanted to bring him back and I said of course. He gave him some oxygen and Keith started looking better. He asked me, which hospital I wanted to take him to and I said Children's Hospital in Boston. When we got to the emergency room at Children's, there was an Arab doctor on call. When she came to see Keith, I said to her Salom Alehhem and she said, "Shalom Aleichem." I believe. and since what Keith had, had been a seizure, she recommended Keppra an anti-seizure medication. Unfortunately, Keith began getting aggressive soon after being prescribed the Keppra. I researched it's side effects and found out that teenagers were apt to become aggressive when put on Keppra. Riverside Community Care offered An Early Intervention Program at three years old. I took him into the Early Intervention Program in Needham, Massachusetts. All they were doing there was playing music all day, music therapy. I said we would have to get him out of there. We had a consultation with someone and they said, "Yes, May Center had a contract through Early Intervention to provide ten hours/week of an ABA program. Keith started it at about two years, six months of age. We got an ABA program at home. They told us that one of the parents would have to be home with him to run the program. I told Janice that we could move back to the apartment, that we could live off my income. She had been at her job for about twelve to fourteen years, twice as long as I'd been at mine and she was earning more than twice as much as I was earning. She said no, she couldn't do it. Whereas, I was used to drastic changes and so I said," Okay, I'll do it."

I had been at Jerry's factory for six years by then. I told him about Keith and I said I need you to lay me off so that I can collect unemployment and go home and take care of him. Jerry said that's going to cost me, but he said okay I'll do it. so I stayed home with Keith.

We hired Frank Robbins, a PhD in Education who specialized with autism and SPED. He observed our ten hour per week ABA therapist, Bridget, from the May Center and said that she wasn't putting the energy in that Keith needed. She was having him do about 10 NVI (non-verbal Imitations) per minute and he needed about 100/minute to get him to speak. So, I jumped in and after a few weeks got his NVI's up to about 100/minute and he started picking up words, but his articulation was not good due to the Dyspraxia that he was suffering from. I took him to an SLP twice a week.

I try not to think about Linda S., the Speech and Language Pathologist in Lexington that I had taken Keith to for about one year, while he was little and doing the ten hours per week ABA program at home. She didn't believe in using primary reinforcers to reward him for speaking only secondary or paradigm rewards.

She couldn't get him to say much. She had him blow bubbles for proper lip movement and blow a recorder or one of those party favors. Finally, after about six months of working with Keith, she went into the break room and got some peanut butter crackers from someone and "bribed him" as she called it, to get Keith to talk. He started to make sounds finally after she started giving him the crackers as a reward for speaking.

So, finally after at least a year with Linda, as Keith's SLP, she wanted to come to the house and give him a session there. In the meantime, I had taught Keith to tell her, "You're fired." When she came to the house, I said to Keith, "What do you want to tell Linda?" And he said, "You're fired" to her. So, that was the end of Linda. What a waste of time she was.

He had an Occupational Therapist (OT) 1x/wk. He had a Play Therapist 1x/wk. He had a PT for a while. We did a ton of articulation drills with him. We got him to pronounce a five-syllable word—refrigerator—okay. Frank Robbins kept saying that he was unintelligible to strangers. People who knew him could understand him, though.

I learned ABA and I went to all kinds of workshops on how to deal with Autism. We finally found out he had Autism. The three components of autism are no social interaction, no creative play and no or poor eye contact. so he had full-blown autism and dyspraxia difficulty speaking. So for six and a half years, I became the educational program manager. I did everything I could. I went to workshops to learn state of the art teaching technology for treating autism.

I went to a behavioral sciences lecture at Cambridge University and everyone was talking about ABA.

We had our first consultant, Alan S., a PhD in psychology who had studied, with some of the people from the Lovaas program. Ivor Lovaas was a PhD from UCLA's early intervention program for children with autism. He had about seven kids that he tested with his early intensive therapy three or four of the seven became normalized the others still had retardation and one eventually became normalized. A normalized child would have/his peers become their therapist. Ivor Lovaas was the guru of ABA at the time. Alan Schnee studied under a fellow from the early autism project and he brought all the program materials plus, he brought two therapists with him that had had experience. Kristen D. and Anjalee N. we had to take a lot of data. When we first had the ABA program it was through early intervention and they contracted with the May Center for ten hours per week.

We had Bridget M. as his therapist. After a couple of months she was teaching non-verbal imitations; like touch head, touch hand, touch nose, etc. we had Frank Robbins as a specialist. He said that she had to get up to 100 NVI limitations per minute before he would become verbal; he said she was too slow and not very ambitious. I stepped in and tried to get him up to 100 non-verbal invitations per minute and he started speaking here and there. He learned all his body parts: his leg, his elbow, etc.

We finally let Bridget go because she wasn't doing well enough. She showed very little enthusiasm. and Ivor Lovaas had recommended a forty-hour-per-week program, not ten.

The most we could do was a thirty-hour per week program because it was five days per week, six hours per day that was thirty and then Janice might do like three hours on Saturdays once and awhile. she didn't want to get into it. she wouldn't even try any of the programs herself; all she did was observe.

There also was a file server specializing in Autism out of the Indiana University at Perdue that I became a member of and every night, after dinner, I would read all the posts for that day and print out any really good ones. There was some discussion about a Gluten Casein food allergy that children with Autism might have. I took specimens from Keith and sent one to the University of Florida that I believe was testing for gluten allergy and the other specimen I believe I sent to the Rocky Mountain Lab where they tested for casein allergy. It turned out that Keith was allergic to gluten and casein. The problem with the Gluten allergy is that the gluten would pass across the blood brain barrier and cause him to be clouded. Typical children had an enzyme in their system to prevent the Gluten from passing into the blood brain barrier.

They hadn't come up with an enzyme supplement at that time yet. I think that there may be one now though.

Bernard Rimland, PhD had a son in California that had Autism and he started the Bernard Rimland Institute for substance testing. He had tested like 100 medications and supplements on children with Autism and had charts indicating the outcomes of using the various substances. I tried a few things like a vitamin from Kirkland Labs and vitamin B-15. The pluses and minuses with Vitamin B-15, if I recall, was that it made Keith speak more and clearly, but after a couple of hours he would crash.

I ended up training the teachers. I hired the Consultants. First we had Alan S., PhD in psychology for the thirty-hour per-week program. Lovaas had recommended a forty-hour week program. He brought the Lovaas program materials to us and he had two previously trained paraprofessionals and I had hired another therapist Christina L. She was brilliant; we paid them about $15 an hour. Each one would do three hours a day. We had three hours per day in the afternoon and three hours per day in the morning so it was six hours per day total. After a year or so, Alan recommended that we send him to NECCA (New England Center for children with Autism). I didn't want to send him there. I had heard some negative things about it. I was getting burnt out. We hired TAP (The Autism Partnership). They had a woman, Kim B. an SLP, she came out of New York. She was a Speech and Language Pathologist who had worked with autism for about twenty-five years. She gave us programs to do with him when she'd visit; which was about every three months. She taught him how to do Imaginary Play, She had some really good ideas on how to help him. After about a year she told us she was moving to the main office in Marin County, California; she was getting married. She said to me why don't you come? I said no I need to stay here with Keith.

Then they brought in this black woman from the autism partnership (TAP) who came in about every three months. She was good and gave us a lot of games to play with Keith.

We had hired this Japanese gal to work in the home ABA program. She was a Speech and Language Therapist. She didn't have her Speech and Language Pathologist Certification yet.

So anyways to make a long story short. She was unbelievably precise in her articulation and she helped Keith improve his articulation dramatically. She needed to do an internship under a Speech and Language Pathologist in order to get her own SLP Certificate. I didn't realize how badly she wanted to get the certification, because after about three months she left us to go to Hawaii and work under an SLP there. In hindsight, I probably could have gotten her a job at Linda S.'s organization in Lexington. Then, she might have been able to continue with Keith part time. One of the things she asked me was how long I thought I could keep the program going at the current energy level and I just shrugged my shoulders and said, "I don't know."

By then, I'd been looking into another program called ABLLS (Assessment of Basic Language and Learning Skills) that had been developed by some psychologists Drs. Sundberg and Partington. They had observed typical kindergarteners and how they develop skills in normal development in tables like bar charts. You started at the beginning and you worked your way up the tower of the bar chart until he became proficient in a skill. From there we went onto another skill if you filled out the entire chart you could normalize your child.

In my research, I found out that Keith had more of a Kanner's type Autism than an Asperger's.

People with Asperger's syndrome are typically very high functioning, but are socially awkward.

Today they get people with Asperger's into social groups, when they are young, to overcome that deficit. I was told that people with Asperger's could sit in an office all day by themselves and write software; I also had heard that the person who had plotted the route to the moon had Asperger's.

We had to fight the school department to provide the home ABA program for thirty to forty hours. We had a PhD in Psychology and a PhD in education and they wrote reports recommending a home ABA program. We brought it to the superintendent of pupil services and they finally approved that they'd pay for the program. Janice did all the accounting for it and I was doing all the educational work. The Superintendent of Pupil Services, Carol D., said that all the kids that they ever help end up with scattered skills. When Keith turned seven we decided to enroll him in kindergarten. We hired a teacher, Paige C. and she would come to the home program once a week in the afternoon, to get caught up in what we were doing at the home program. Then she was supposed to generalize the skills that Keith was learning at home into the school environment.

When Keith was eight, he went to first grade and we hired Ellen D. to be his aid at school. He was going to the Bowen School and they gave us a closet to do 1:1 therapy with him. We trained Ellen at the home program and then she'd do an hour or so of ABA at school per day at school. I set up the closet with a table, a couple of chairs and a little two or three drawer table to store his learning materials in.

I had hired Leslie D., a person who had an MS in Sped with twenty-five years of experience and she was going to be our consultant for the ABLLS program. We knew what skills we needed to teach him, but we didn't know how to teach them. We could use her experience to teach us how. Working with Leslie was like pulling teeth. She had a bad attitude. She said that the Newton Public Schools only gave her six hours per month to consult, whereas Medfield, had given her ten to fifteen together with Ipswich who was giving her ten to twelve hours per month. Towards the end of kindergarten, Leslie started showing up late for our team meetings. I asked her what the problem was, but she wouldn't say. Finally, one day she showed up late and started playing with her phone instead of leading the team. I got angry and said to her, "If you don't want to participate, why don't you leave?" So, she replied," I thought that you didn't need me. I said, "Of course we need you. We don't know how to teach a lot of these things to him and you do." So, she stayed and I kept pulling teeth from her.

We did a lot of articulation drills with him. The problem was keeping everything in maintenance.

After first grade was over, the administrators wanted to meet. Carol D., Superintendent of Pupil Services, Robin F., Inclusion Facilitator, and Mozelle B., Director of Special Education were at the meeting, Leslie D., our home consultant, was also present. I had analyzed the work done at school during kindergarten and the work we had done in the home program that year using the ABLLS as a guide. The kindergarten had only taught him about 5–6 percent of their goals and we at home had achieved 85–90 percent of our goals and believe me we had many more goals at home than the kindergarten had.

Carol D. asked Leslie if she thought that she could do the same thing that the home- and public-school program were doing in the school under one roof. Leslie replied, "Yes." I stood up outraged and said, "I can't believe that you are even considering this when we achieved 85–90 percent of our goals at home and the kindergarten had only achieved 5–6 percent of their goals and we had many more goals at home then the kindergarten had. All the bureaucrats just became quiet and the meeting ended.

Well, a few weeks later, we received the IEP for Keith and they were trying to get rid of the home program. I was a bit burnt out and Janice didn't want to use the dining room as a classroom anymore, she wanted to use it for entertaining. So, ignorantly, I agreed to the IEP with the stipulation that they provide him with an ABA program similar to the one we were providing at home. Later, I spoke to another family who had gone through the process before, and they said that I should have written" Stay Put" on the IEP, then the school would have had to take us to court to stop us from continuing his combination program. Janice signed off on the IEP and approved it.

The public school system gave Leslie 25 hours of consulting fees up front for consultation during July and August. The teachers that she was supposed to consult to said that she only showed up for six hours the entire two months.

When Keith was two years old under Governor William Weld, Chapter 766, the Massachusetts Education law guidelines stated that a special needs student "would get a maximum feasible education." When Paul Tsongas. got in as governor, he changed the law to be equal to the federal law which stated that the special needs student would get a free and feasible education. WHO would determine what was feasible and it would become minimum feasible, because no one really cared. There had been about six states who had had "maximal feasible." The rest of the states went according to the Federal guidelines.

I tried to win Mozelle over by bringing her a notebook in which I had performed an analysis of kindergarten goals and how many were satisfied and home program goals and how many were fulfilled. She just took the notebook and put it in her desk drawer and ignored it.

For the summer after kindergarten, they had paid Leslie about twenty-five hours upfront to consult and train the person who was going to be Keith's first grade aide, Michelle S. Well, I felt that Ellen D. could help with the training, because we had pretty thoroughly trained her and with Leslie going in to train Michelle over the summer, I felt like I could stay away. It turned out that Leslie only showed up twice for about six hours total during the summer months. She wasn't showing up and they had paid her up front, so she made off like a bandit. After the summer school, Robin laughed and said to me, "You should let Leslie take you out to dinner."

I ended up designing a website for Jerry's company using Pagemill and studying HTML and SHTML that summer. When Keith came home from School, I would work on teaching him how to read. I figured if I could teach him how to read, he would pretty much be able to teach himself anything.

I had a lot of computer games for Keith to play with. I got a touch screen so he could make choices. All he had to do was point to an Icon and it would give an audible output and he could make a choice that way.

Well, Keith developed about 125 expressive words that he had articulated pretty well and also about 250–300 receptive words. I was told that a child only needs to have about 500 words to get by.

He could also answer questions with a full sentence when given a sentence stem such as, Q." What do you see?" A. I see ______", Q. What do you want?, A. I want ________Q. What do you have? A. I have ________"

We also did intraverbals as part of the ABLLS program. Examples:

Q. Why do you use a refrigerator? A. to keep things cold'

Q. Name 3 things that a house has A. A roof, door and windows

Q. Name 3 things that a car has. A. an engine, doors and windows.

We had about three pages of these and we tried to keep them in maintenance.

In second grade, they wanted to send him to the Countryside School. I should have fought them because we lived on the east side of Beacon Street, he should have gone to the Angiers School in Waban. The Angier school had SLP's who had aids doing articulation drills and it was a higher quality school. All the lawyers and doctors lived in that district.

Rachele T. was the Head Teacher for the special needs classroom at the Countryside School. Rachel T. just wanted to be a behavior therapist. She really didn't want to be a teacher. We first met her when she was training at NECCA. I had noticed that all she did at NECCA was keep looking around the room to see what was going on. I didn't like her from the very beginning. She gave me a bad impression when she was at NECCA. Keith had been there for about three to six months, after I got burnt out. NECCA was just cookie cutting the kids out. The Program Director, Rene` M. had given me a tour and I noted that they were teaching the same exact thing to each student. I didn't like it. It was like making robots. It was hateful and they had a residential program. After the kids went through their program they would just stick them in their residences; so, they wouldn't teach them much at all.

The way NECCA worked was that they had these teachers just out of school, not knowing anything and they would train them on the program first and then the teacher would train the student on the program. The first teacher that Keith had was Amy B. She was like a whirlwind. Very energetic, which is what Keith needed. They had quite a few bikes in the gym area and I asked her if she could teach him how to ride a bicycle. she said, "Oh, yes." She never taught him anything, so I went in there I was outraged with them and I talked to the CEO of the school and I told him I didn't want him in there anymore and he said either we don't observe the program anymore or we take him home; So we brought him back home. By then, the ABLLS (Assessment of Basic Language and Learning Skills) had been developed.

So, they sent him to the countryside School. Rachelle T., trained at NECCA was the head teacher. As I mentioned, she was at NECCA when I went in to observe Keith. I noticed that all she did was observe what was going on around her. I was totally demoralized. Here was a person who had no interest in teaching, only doing behavioral analysis. She wanted to become a BCBA (Board Certified Behavior Analyst).

At about seven years of age, I found this Speech & Language Pathologist out of Wellesley. Gabriel M. was her name. All she did was give me drills to do with Keith. She wouldn't do much with him. I don't think that she wanted to get her hands dirty. She was a real pain in the ass. She gave me homework every week.

When Keith was nine years old, the Newton Public School hadn't delivered services that were in the IEP. I put a Pro Se lawsuit on Newton for two million dollars for the damages to him. The services that they said they're going to provide, but they didn't. I did it Pro Se; that way I wouldn't have to follow the rules of the court to the letter, but I did study the court's terminology. I requested a jury by my peers. I got a document back from the school system lawyers saying that I'd have to bring it back before the special needs association. I didn't think that was necessary because they said, when you file Pro Se, you don't have to follow the law to the T. I was too burnt out to go before the Special Needs people. I was saving my energy for the court trial.

So the way things turned out, Carol D., like I said, they'd be taking care of him for the rest of his life, instead of him being independent at 2 million dollars would have let him be independent and now it's going to be used for supervisors and caregivers for the rest of his life that's pretty much the way they saw it.

I went to Vincent Carbone's Workshop. He had a PhD in Education and came up with his own program. He was just using flash cards a lot to get the kids communicative. It was rapid flashing of cards instead of nonverbal imitation. It was receptive language and expressive language in rapid succession. It was thought that that you could jump the student. When I first started out in the program one of the pitfalls of having a home ABA program was that you need to hire about 7 therapists in advance and train all of them because there was going to be attrition. The girl Megan on the file server that I belonged to was getting normalized; they had a forty-hour per week ABA program and had hired about seven paraprofessional therapists to work with her from the beginning.

My life since then has been all ups and downs. When I was taking care of Keith in the afternoon after school, as I stated earlier Janice said that she didn't want to use our dining room as a school room anymore; she wanted to use it for entertaining, which she never did until four or five years later.

I moved out within two weeks, after she said she didn't want to use the dining room as a classroom anymore. I didn't want to hit her or anything. Keith came to me in the afternoons, since I had co-legal and co- physical custody of him. I moved to Brighton for five years, a residential neighborhood and I would see Keith after school and I tried to teach him how to read. I spent probably seven years trying to teach him how to read with no success. I think one of the things that would have been better early on, was if I had taught him how to read instead of trying to teach him how to speak. I developed my own program to teach him how to read and he was making progress, but then after a certain point when a child reaches about age thirteen the brain hardens and it's not that malleable anymore. I think, if I had taught him how to read early on he would have been able to learn anything that he wanted to; so, that's something to think about. I had him in the afternoons. in the mornings I was free there were no part time jobs at that time so I began going back to Elliott House which was the follower to Second Story this time it was an international Clubhouse certified and it was a very structured program and I had company. I was a single dad at the time which was very unusual.

Keith and Me

I got some temporary employment positions from Elliot House. The first one was as a filing clerk for about 12 hours per week at Maloney properties in Wellesley. They managed about 120 complexes and I did all the filing for them for their invoices. I did it for a few months it was very boring I got bored stiff, so one Friday I told my supervisor I was leaving it's my last day so my supervisor got angry with me and she gave me a bunch of pink paperwork to work with, as if she was firing me even though I told her I was leaving that day. I went and did the filing anyways f*** her. I remember that day I left, but a year later I went back there because I wanted a TE job again and it was the same s*** but, I did a six-month commitment and then Jeff C. took over and he just milked the job for what it was worth. He stayed there for years, milking and milking.

I got a TE job as a Page at the library; filing books and helping patrons. It was the most boring job that I've ever had, but I had a six-month commitment; so, I was going to finish up the six-month commitment and then give my notice, Alan L. the supervisor said he was surprised that I wasn't staying, he was hoping that I was going to stay as a Supported Employment Position, but I told him no, I just had a six-month commitment and that was it. So then I went out on my own.

My bills were piling up so before the library job, I had to sell my car because I couldn't afford to pay for brakes, the assessment tax and new inspection sticker; so, I sold my car and for two years I used the T, the Ride and the Newton Senior vouchers.

I got a job at a place called IRS in Porter Square, Cambridge. We raised funds for Democratic institutions like the Democratic National Convention, Anti-Gun Lobby, Democratic Governors' Association.

I wrote my own scripts. They trained us in fundraising. There were three steps. The first ask, the second ask, the third ask, etc.

So, one day the Ride was supposed to pick me up and take me to work. It was on Marathon Monday. I told the dispatcher that Washington Street was closed due to the Boston Marathon and that they would have to come through Auburndale. Up Lexington Street onto Grove Street, take a left on Cornell Street then a right on to Moulton Street and I'd be at the bottom of Moulton Street. The driver couldn't figure out how to get to me and kept getting lost. It took four or five hours before he arrived and by then the barricades had been taken down for the marathon. Luckily, I had started to go to work early enough, so that I wasn't late. If you were late they closed the doors and they wouldn't let you in.

So, after two years of hoofing it without a car, I stopped by Santander bank on the way to a dealership and had them check whether I'd be able to qualify for an auto loan. They said that I would and the salesman at Rte. 2 Hyundai in Leominster told me over that phone that he'd be able to get me single digit financing. Of course, he lied and my monthly payments were about $400 for an Accent. I had fair credit. I had had a bankruptcy; the loan interest rate from Santander was high and the sales manager told me to make sure that I paid my first three months payments on time, then, go to a credit union and instead of financing for five years, finance it for seven years so my payments would be lower.

I paid the bill on time for three months and then got the RTN federal Credit Union to refinance it for seven years instead of the five through Santander. I stretched it out to eighty-four months of payments for $286 per month. Five years into owning that car, I had two more years to pay it off and I totaled it. I was behind a pickup truck and I was looking at his back compartment and I noticed some equipment and I was like kind of looking at the equipment trying to figure out what it was, I realized it was a high-pressure jet spray to clean a house or something like that. I looked to the right of him and there was a lane open and so, I went to take that lane and he must have just stopped and I hit his bumper. I put a little dent on his bumper, but my car was pretty smashed in and so they towed it away. I went to the place where they towed it and drove it to Haskins Auto in Wellesley to have the body work done on it; but, when the appraiser got there he met with me and told me that the car was totaled. He couldn't believe that I had driven it to Haskins; so we worked out a deal. I got some of my equity back in the car, I went out and I bought a Toyota Corolla at Bernardi Toyota in Framingham. The monthly payments are about $20 more a month than the Hyundai was. The sad part, as I noted, was that in two more years, I would have owned the Hyundai free and clear.

For the next couple of weeks, I was socializing with people who smoked and I kept saying, "I haven't smoked in over thirty years," "I haven't smoked in over thirty years," and after a couple of weeks, I asked one of the fellows whether I could buy two cigarettes for a dollar. He said, "Sure" and ever since then I've been up and running for about five years. Three months on and three months off. It's a tough habit to break, once it's started. I've gone to an in-person Nicotine Anonymous meeting for a couple of years weekly, pre-pandemic. I've done the NicAnon conference calls. I pretty much tried everything. I tried the NRT products, i.e., Nicotine gum, lozenges, and patches.

none of them really worked for me and they aren't cheap. Plus, when I researched the negative effects of Nicotine, I found out that it constricts your blood vessels. That sure doesn't sound good. I used 1-800-Quit-Now seven times before. This was my 8th time with them. They provide seven coaching calls and NRT merchandise for eight weeks. This time, I stopped without the NRT stuff and it's been twenty-eight days so far. The first two coaching calls explained to me what I was going through. They told me that even if I hadn't smoked in over thirty years, the first cigarette I smoked would excite a section of my brain that secreted Dopamine. What a rude awakening. Then, when I spoke with my doctor and he confirmed what they said and told me that I could get the same dopamine release by exercising. Well, I've been exercising and I still have the urge to smoke. Even right now, I want to have a cigarette. But, I know that one cigarette is too much and 1000 are not enough. It's a fool's game. I'm going to try not to be a fool.

So now I'm broke. I have no job. I was doing DoorDash, You earn like $11–15 an hour and after auto expenses it comes down to about $8–$12 per hour, below minimum wage $14 + /hr. There was a class action suit against them about that, but I didn't participate because I thought I didn't want to get my new partner pissed off. Between smoking cigarettes and driving for DoorDash I just can't make ends meet, so I'm going to have to sell my Toyota Corolla and get a cheaper car. The reason I can't use my Toyota Corolla for Uber (which pays more) is that the front seat upholstery is dirty and stained plus the trunk is full and when you do Uber they want the trunk to be empty and your upholstery to be clean.

Steve C., the new Director at Elliot House, told me he had a job for me as an office assistant, (maybe someday Keith could do it) and then I waited about three weeks and he told me that they were thinking about going in a different direction Well, I just spoke with Steve C. and he said that it sounds pretty positive that they're going to have a new TE in parallel with Jeff C. at Adelson. He told me that I was the first candidate for the position.

So, Tami at Adelson, sent Steve the job description at the end of January. Due to illnesses and vacations, I finally had a meet and greet with Tami T. and Steve G., in the middle of March and they gave me a tour and both were nice to me. I got to ask questions after the tour. Then they sent me the paperwork for processing. I had to agree to a Credit check, a Cori check, and a drug test. About three weeks later, I was sent in for a drug test. In addition to a urine specimen, they took a few hair specimens. It's been seven days since the specimens were taken and I'm waiting for the results. I read that it could take two to three weeks for the drug test on the hair specimens. I'm wondering when we're going to get those results back.

In the meantime, Linda K., a neighbor of mine, and I have gone to flea markets and yard sales. At the church in West Newton, I bought a pair of dress shoes for $4 and a paper shredder for $3. We went to see a movie at the Needham Senior Center. We've gone on a couple of walks. We went to a comedy show last week and we went out for dinner. We go out for coffee. She's had Tea at my place a couple of times. She claims she's depressed her apartment is scattered with paper on the floor. I told her that it's only a five to six-hour job to clean it up, but she doesn't want to do it.

The person that introduced me to the Golda Meir House, as my buddy, was Leslie. She was very nice. It turns out she has MS. She is very, very friendly. She loves everybody here. She knows a lot of people here. She walks with a rollabrator, an upright walker she's always at the Tuesday and Thursday Julia's Café I can call her anytime I want to talk.

The only thing wrong with this place is it's for people sixty-two and older people. A lot of people are in their eighties or nineties and some of them have dementia. It's sad I met one woman, who is like ninety-five years old and she has no memory, but she's in excellent physical shape; no walker, no cane. Most of the women in their eighties have walkers.

I went to my rabbi's son's Bar Mitzvah a couple of weeks ago and I was down to, like all I could give was a gift of $18 which is just a token of life " have a good life." I can't really afford to go to many of those functions anymore because I lack funding.

Well one of the best things about this place is that we get a new book to read about once a month for the book club. Most of the people in the book club are elderly and just aren't with it. The leader of the group is a retired librarian, named Natalie, and she's pretty good. The last book we read, "Britt Marie was Here." by Jojo Moyes was awful, but Natalie put a positive spin on it.

"Birds of a Feather" was good, but I found a flaw in it and she immediately recognized what I told her about it and agreed that I had found a flaw.

I got turned on to Daniel Silva by my friend Susan F., another resident, She reads books in the designated smoking area. I read one of his entitled *Portrait of a Spy* the other was *A Death in Vienna* and they're pretty good and then the third book I got was about Islamic militant terrorist bombers and I decided that there's enough of that in the real world, I don't have to read about it in a book of fiction. So, I stopped reading his books for a while. Susan told me that he comes out with a new book once per year in August. Two of his books were supposed to be made into movies, but that hasn't happened yet.

My ex-wife lent me a book to read entitled, *Red Notice* by William Browder. It had been lent to her by a friend. It was excellent; it was about this guy who went to Russia and, with twenty-five million dollars of seed money, he raised over five billion dollars and uncovered the thirteen Oligarch families that were corrupt and controlled most of the businesses in Russia. Initially they were looked upon poorly by Putin, but then they started paying him off and he accepted the money. Instead of the money going into the government for the people, it was going into his pocket and made him probably the richest man on Earth. The book entailed one of the author's associates being murdered by the Russians. They wanted him to admit to some lie about the corruption in Russia and he refused. So, they put him into prisons that were worse and worse, worser, and worser until they beat the hell out of him and killed him. His name was Magnitsky and they wrote the Magnitsky act after him. In other words no Russians that had anything to do with Magnitsky's death including, oligarchs, judges, prison, etc. could have visas or passports to the United States or do any business in the United States. Putin was really angry about that and he stopped Americans from being able to adopt children from Russia.

The Russian people were angry with Putin about that and there were protests in the streets.

Putin had the courts decide that Bill Browder was wanted for Tax Evasion and Putin still wants him back in Russia to stand trial. About two years ago, Bill Browder was in Spain and when he was going through customs, they stopped him. It appeared that Russia had a Red Notice out on him with Interpol (the international police) to have him deported to Russia. Putin still wants him dead. Bill Browder used all his contacts in the media to get the Red Notice dropped and to get himself released. After what happened with Magnitsky, he decided to give up his family, his business and devote his life to doing good to try and balance out evil in the world.

Family Ties

The only grandparent I had growing up was my mother's father. His wife had passed away from pancreatic cancer before I was born. His daughter died of nephritis at the age of seventeen. That was before I was born. I had a great-uncle named Uncle Louie who was my mother's brother. He had two siblings. But the only one I knew was my aunt Fanny who had been a seamstress. My uncle took care of her when she got older and I saw her just before she died. She was in a lot of pain and she was in agony. My uncle took care of her until she passed. My uncle took care of his brother too, before he passed away. My great-uncle was one of the last gentlemen in his generation. My uncle Georgie was my mother's brother who lived in California and I only saw him twice in my life. He came to my nephew's wedding one of the times.

My family used to go to Fields Park in Brockton a lot when I was growing up. There was a beautiful grove where we could barbecue, and a beach area where we could swim. The parents could watch the kids swimming to make sure that they were okay. Sooky and Hy used to come with Jackie and Anita and I'm not sure whether Victor came. They are distant cousins of ours on my aunt Celia's side. Her husband was my father's uncle and Sooky was Aunt Celia's sister. So, we were distant cousins, but we adopted them as family because we had such a tiny family. Anita's got a few kids and grandkids and she's doing well for herself. I haven't talked to her in a couple of years. She's usually busy with her friends when I call.

Growing up, all I had was my sister Barbara, who is four years older than me. My mother worked part time. I had to follow my sister around with her friends while my mother was at work. Some of her friends and I didn't get along very well. My mother was a Cub Scout leader for the Boy Scouts and the den mother for the Girl Scouts. I had to attend all my sister's Girl Scout events and I remember at the school where they met I was sitting playing with blocks, building towers and then knocking them down the whole time they had their meeting. I recall when I had to go with them on a field trip to the Arnold Arboretum to pick leaves. They would press the leaves between two pieces of Saran Wrap and put them in a book and identify them. That's how I learned a lot about what type of leaves they were.

Whenever my parents were out of the house my sister and I fought. They would come home and punish us both. I remember one time, when my sister threw her slipper at me and I ducked and it went through the storm window and broke it. My folks came home and they told us that we would both have to pay for it but both of us shared the guilt even though my sister had thrown her slipper at me.

My sister married Steven, the manager of an automobile dealership in Central Square. He learned how to lie a lot because he'd have to lie to his customers. My sister had to deal with it. He lied to her and she told him that he couldn't lie to her anymore and that he had to be honest with her, even though he was a liar at work. My sister learned how to lie from him.

She taught kindergarten for about seven years in East Cambridge. It was a ghetto area with a project and most of her pupils were from the project. The kids used to slash the teachers' tires and so my brother-in-law would bring her to school and take her home after. Some of the mothers were prostitutes and one day when my brother-in-law went to pick up my sister, he was solicited by a third grader. My brother-in-law was working nearby in Central Square and so he would pick her up and take her home from work. One time my sister had a kindergartener try to attack her with scissors. So after six or seven years of that, she decided to have her own family and take care of her own kids instead of other people's kids.

I had moved to New Orleans by then and I flew up for each child's birth. She had a son and a daughter, Adam and Judith. When Adam was being born, my brother-in-law was in the operating room with my sister and she started turning green. He said to the doctor, "Looks like she's dying, do something." So they went into the emergency procedure during a C-section so that she wouldn't die from toxemia. My sister was tough, though. She didn't want her children to be four years apart like we had been. She wanted them to have the same peers.

So when she got to the recovery room after the C-section she said to the people in the recovery room, "I'll be back next year." She's a tough cookie, even though she almost died. I was anointed Adam's Godfather at his bris. I had to be present when he got circumcised by the mohel.

When Adam was little, I bought him a Commodore 64 and tried to teach him how to program it in Basic. He never caught on. I don't know why. Maybe it just wasn't for him. Judy got a dollhouse from one of the prisons and I built a table for it so it could roll around the room and would be higher up so she could play with it. I was also doing some stained-glass work and I made Judy a Strawberry Short-cake and my nephew a Tin Soldiers so they could hang them in their windows. I used to go out on bike rides with my nephew. My niece Judy is very, very smart. When the kids she was growing up with in high school were doing drugs, she had gotten a whole stack of library books on the drugs they were taking and read books about them instead of ever taking them.

My brother-in-law, Steven, my sister's husband, taught my sister how to lie, cheat, and steal. My sister Barbara is a liar, cheat, and a thief. When my mother was alive, she told my sister that as long as she kept her out of the nursing home, she would give her house to Barbara. My brother-in-law is a car salesman. He convinced my folks to give the house to their daughter. They still put her in the nursing home. I haven't seen my sister in over three years and she only lives two towns over from where I live. She won't see me. My nephew, who also lives two towns over hasn't communicated with me. The last time I saw them was at a family reunion in Framingham about seven or eight years ago. My nephew is the general manager at Toyota Watertown. He's a killer. Even when he was younger, he had to cheat at Monopoly; he could never lose. I speak with my sister about once a week and all she does is try to dump her problems on me.

I have suffered through autism and epilepsy and dyspraxia and they haven't seen Keith in years. I got an invitation recently to their granddaughter's bat mitzvah and their grandson's bar mitzvah. It's in June of 2022 that's about seven months away. They are standing on such ceremonies that I won't be able to see any of them for seven months. My niece, living in my parents' former house in Newton Highlands, is in the same town as I live in. But I'd only gotten one invite to her house, about fifteen years ago. My sister says that I have addictive behaviors and I go from smoking, to drinking, to smoking pot.

When my mother and father were alive, they decided to divide the house in which my sister would get a 1/5th, nephew and niece would get 1/5th each, my son would get 1/5th and I would get a 1/5th. That meant that my son would get $100,000, I would get $100,000, my sister would get $100,000, and my niece and nephew would get $100,000 each. They reneged on keeping my mother out of the nursing home. My mother was in the nursing home for a couple of years until she passed from natural causes. I went to see her a couple of times, but she was in such a degraded shape, I couldn't stand it. She asked me to feed her grapes. I couldn't stand seeing her in such a debilitated way, so I stopped visiting.

My father on the other hand was a prick. In the end he told me not to trust my sister and not to believe a word she said. He hated my brother-in-law for what he did to the house. My sister has a house down the cape in North Dennis. She's had it for years but has never even invited me to it. She also has a condo in Florida. She's never invited me there either.

My brother-in-law, Steven, is a wicked cheat and liar. I guess you have to be that when you sell cars for a living. I had an associate that was looking for a new Toyota, so I sent her to my nephew Adam. I told my sister and she said not to send her to Adam to send her to Steven.

She said my nephew doesn't have time. He's too busy managing the dealerships. When I got a card for my great-niece's and great-nephew's ban mitzvah, I googled the address and found out that my nephew had a mansion in Needham.

A couple of years ago, I tried to track down my first cousins in Israel. One's name is Label and the other one, I think, is Dora. When the Soviet Union collapsed, they were living in Poland and were afraid that they would be subjected to pogroms again. My father's brother had passed away. All he had done was drive a cab for his job because he had been blacklisted by the Soviets. He wouldn't comply with communism. He was a refusenik. He kept a gun with him. They arrested him once because he had a gun. They took away the gun and put him in jail. They blacklisted him, so all he could get was a job as a cab driver.

My father wanted to bring them over to this country (sponsor them), but his wife didn't want to come because she had one son in college studying and the daughter was raising a family, but when the Soviet Union collapsed, they tried to get into the US, but the quota was full. My cousin Taeble, whose husband was a diamond cutter (and died at a very young age) has a lot of money and set them up in Israel with an apartment.

My Love Life

My first crush was on Sandy Fleischman. I liked her a lot. She was pretty. The only problem was she liked my neighbor Vicky S. better. That was my first hurt when I was about ten years old.

My second crush was on Shelly F., but we lived at distance from each other so I never got to see her; so it faded away.

In high school my girlfriend was Bonnie T. I f***** that up when I went to a Northeastern frat party on a Friday night with Jerry G., and she thought I was picking up girls; so, she got drunk and in the backseat of my neighbor's car was making out with him.

In college we used to go out to the happy hours on Fridays and I met this girl Debbie that I liked a lot she was hot we used to go to the drive-in theaters on the weekends, but wouldn't have sex we would go on humping and humping each other. I'd be massaging her. She said to me you should be a rabbi, because I think she wanted me to lay her, but I wouldn't. I didn't want to get her pregnant. She was hot. I used to perspire so much when I was out with her it was unbelievable. She was working as an administrative assistant or something when I was in school, she lived in Weymouth. She wanted to see me every day, but I couldn't because I was doing both programs, the Bachelor's and the Master's program at the same time. I had to study. I told her I liked seeing her on the weekends, but she wanted more. and she just kind of broke up with me and I was very upset. So, I drove to her house in Weymouth and I was going to tell her that I was going to quit school and do something else. I'd get a job and settle down with her. Her mother came to the door and said she wasn't home. I looked up into the window and there she was on the second floor looking out the window.

In college, my girlfriend was Bonnie B. She was one of the waitresses at the Brighams where I worked as a part-time night manager. She was in the class behind me majoring in physical education. I went to some of her gymnastic sessions. She was quite something with a parallel bar—wow. I have never had sex before and I wanted to with Bonnie, but she wanted to wait till she got married.

One night, when I was working as night manager, I was really wound up at the end of the shift. As usual we had to put everything away and I had to wash the floors and count out the money and make the bank deposit. So, I was really wound up. It was about 11:00 p.m. when I got out, so I went across the street with two of the girls that had been waitressing that night and we got drunk. They told me I was too drunk to drive home, but I could stay in their dorm room. One of them told me I could sleep in her bed with her.

I had my pants on and was going to sleep. She said you can take your pants off if you want, so, I took my pants off and I started kissing her and massaging her breasts and she said to me you know what's going to happen next. I had heard she was a little loose and I said, "Yeah, I think so," so she stood up and dropped her nightgown and got on top of me and we had sex. It was the first time I ever had sex and then after that she said to me, "You know you're pretty good." I said, "Thanks." We discussed it as just a platonic relationship and we agreed.

Lo and behold her roommate was the best friend of my girlfriend, Bonnie, and the next day she told her how I had sex with her roommate, Rosalie. Bonnie was upset that day and I said to her I'm sorry I just wanted to experiment and have sex. I'm twenty-one years old and I haven't had sex yet. Then she said, "Well, you can have it with me, then if you want," so I said okay so we had it and everything was okay, but she was very very tight as if there was like a bone in the way. Whenever I inserted my penis in her, it hurt. I don't know if it hurt her too, but it hurt me.

I thought I loved her. She wanted to get married. I said, "Let's wait till you graduate college. I'll wait for you. It's only one year." So anyways, I don't think her mother was too happy with her seeing a Jewish guy. She took her away to White Horse Beach for the summer and when she came back, Bonnie didn't seem to be the same. Something was different and I kind of had had it with the relationship anyways because it hurt having sex with her. We didn't discuss anything about the pain.

One night when a friend of mine was participating in community theater as one of the actors, I had bought tickets. I purchased tickets and I told her what time she had to be at my parents' house by and she didn't show up on time. She actually showed up about a half hour late. I was steaming. It gave me a good excuse to get rid of her. I told her to get the f*** out of my house and I never wanted to see you again. You f***** up my whole night. So she got in her car and she took off and we never spoke again. I did see her in passing one day when I was on campus and I didn't talk to her and she didn't talk to me. She had said to me that I was going crazy with the accelerated program that I was in.

When I graduated college I think that on Christmas I got a Christmas card from Debbie. I guess she probably had waited for me to get out of college and maybe start things up again. I was ready to go out and conquer the world. I disregarded the card and just put it in the back of my memory.

When I lived in the new apartment complex in New Orleans on Eden Street, I met an elderly woman named Joey M. She had been a debutante when she was younger and she had all the ways about her, but she was poor now and she worked in an insurance agency and every night she had to have her bottle of Punch and get high. We became great friends and she made me dinner once in a while. She told me that I have the manners of royalty and that I could eat at anybody's table. She fixed me up with her next-door neighbor, Patty, who was a nurse and had polio from birth. She was the first person who ever had polio that became a nurse. Patty was very smart. She and I had some fun times. We went out for dinner, all clean fun. Patty was from Baton Rouge; her parents lived there. We went there once and visited with them.

Her father was watching a football game and he had me join in with him. I proposed to Patty and she accepted. I was accepted as far as they were concerned, but my mother and my sister told me they wouldn't go to a church wedding. The only problem was I had done a lot of running around in the French Quarter chasing after prostitutes and hooking up, and so I thought I might have cerebral syphilis. I went to see a doctor when I had a little bit of a fever. I did have a little pimple on my penis, which indicated syphilis. I was so depressed. I didn't care if I was just going to die from the syphilis. I read that in the fourth stage of syphilis you die. When I did go to the doctor because I had a little fever, I asked him if I had syphilis and he said maybe gonorrhea and gave me an antibiotic. Patty wanted to have sex, but I told her I might have syphilis and I didn't want to do it. I didn't want to give her syphilis.

I didn't seek treatment until I got a wedding invitation to Olivia and Kenny's wedding. I had to RSVP by August 31, my birthday. It dawned on me how much I loved Olivia and so I wanted to live and get to see her again.

My mother told me to take Patty to a rabbi. I took Patty to a rabbi and I identified with him so much that I realized that I loved Judaism. Well, it split me down the middle. That's when I got sick.

One time when I lived on Eden Street, the end of my street was Fat City. It was like all kinds of dance clubs and bars. At the end of my street there was a bar that I would frequent to see if I could pick anybody up, but never had any luck. One night I went in by myself; a little later and I had three or four margaritas. And it was getting late and I said to the bartender who was a woman. "Do you always get your customers this drunk?" And she kind of laughed and said, "Oh hey," but I asked her when she was getting off work and she said in about fifteen to twenty minutes. I asked her if she wanted to go out dancing and she said, "Yes, sure" so we went out dancing and then went back to my apartment. I don't know what happened after that, I kind of blacked out, but in the morning when I woke up, she was gone. So the next day, I went back to the bar that she worked at. I asked about her and they said that she forgot about her babysitter the night before and didn't get home till two to three in the morning. She was afraid she'd lose custody of her child so she quit the job.

There were a couple of nurses in my complex, Richard and his wife Joelle were there. They're very nice people and they introduced me to margaritas they would make them on the weekends when they were off duty. He worked in the ICU and she worked in the CCU and they would get stressed out, so they would like to have a nice time on the weekends. They brought over their cousin Klein J. and he and I became good friends. There was something weird about Klein. He was very handsome and he took me out to his family's house across from Lake Pontchartrain. They had 750 acres of land, which they weren't farming because the government was paying them not to. His father was just doing electrician work, I guess to pay the taxes.

Klein set up a tent when we were in the woods somewhere and I was kind of attracted to him and wanted to see what it was like to have anal sex. He had anal sex with me. I was a little satisfied but not much and I decided it wasn't for me. He had a friend from college come by one weekend and the three of us lay down on the grass and we were jerking each other off. I asked his close friend whether he was gay, but he had been Klein's roommate in college. He was married, but told me he'd done some homosexual stuff with Klein when they were in college. After that I decided it wasn't for me. I experimented with it. It was clear he was a great guy. I realized later in life he probably had Asperger's Syndrome. He was some kind of a savant because he showed me some very advanced statistics from school that he was doing.

Since I've gotten sick, I've had a few girlfriends. One of them was Jesse Fuller. Beautiful as a goddess, she was trying to write the next great American novel. She had, like, a 354-page manuscript. We hung out together she took me to see her father on his ranch up in Manchester. He had owned Peter Fuller Cadillac-Olds in Brookline and her grandfather had been the governor of Massachusetts. We visited her mother at Assisted Living. Her father and mother were separated or divorced. We went to her mother's house. No one was living there. It was all furnished and didn't seem that anyone had lived there for a while. We went to her aunt's house around Manchester by the ocean. The air up there was so f****** clean. It was unbelievable, not like in the city. Jessie and I hung around probably for a couple of years. Like I said she's very very fussy. One-time we were hanging out in front of a pharmacy store because she wanted to get medication for me to stay overnight. The pharmacist wouldn't give it to her so she threw a shit fit inside. The police came by and they confronted her for blocking the entrance and she went to hit the cop who took her dog, Cherub. The cop arrested her for assault. Her dog, Cherub, was prone to seizures and she was very upset.

I didn't know what to do, so I just left and went home. I called her brother, Peter, the next day. I asked him if he wanted me to pick her up. He said, "No, I'm picking her up" and I said, "Okay I'll meet you." For whatever reason he kind of blew me off. Jesse was a poor girl. Her father wanted her to work. She got a job working at the Dress Barn in Framingham. She was a good sales girl. She loved to talk people into buying clothes for themselves. We both never had much money. One time she borrowed $50 from me to get her nephew a gift. I told her later that she owed me $50. She said, "No, I don't." I went to play it on my recording on my phone. I had it saved as a voicemail and she said don't do that. She was really just a poor little rich girl.

Her father on the ranch had a woman taking care of him. He was fighting to his dying day to get the Kentucky Derby trophy that his horse had won years earlier. His horse had been found to take an NSAID and it was illegal at the time for them to do that. So, they had disqualified his horse. Now it's legal for them to give a horse an NSAID. Until the day he died, he had his lawyers fighting to get the Kentucky Derby trophy back.

I'm not sure what he died of because he was sick when I met him. I think he had a blood clot in his leg(s) because they said they were doing the final thing they could do, which was attach leeches to him to suck the blood out; that's all I knew.

I didn't stay with Jesse after her father passed or even give her any support.

I heard that she had moved to New York and was living in a $2,000 a month apartment. She probably had inherited money from her father and now she's trying to work on creating an American novel in New York.

I met this girl Linda A. at a New Year's Eve party that a friend of mine Louise threw at a Chinese restaurant and we hit it off right away. She was pretty and sweet. I said, "I'll give you a ride home if you want." She said, "Okay, that would be great." I gave her a ride home and then I called on her. It turned out she was a childhood diabetic and she was forty years old. They were giving her a special party at the diabetes center because she made it to forty without problems.

We went out to see a movie once and then we went over to a shopping mall. When we got home, we talked and we'd french kiss and I loved it. I fell in love with her—head over heels. She asked me to buy something for her at the shopping center, I refused, but I think because of the fact that I cheaped out and wouldn't buy a pair of shoes for her at the mall, she dumped me. I decided she was a bit of a gold digger and decided that she didn't want to go out with me anymore. I loved her, though. I really fell in love with her.

From there, I moved on to Danielle C. I had been with her a couple of years earlier and we were trying to have sex and I couldn't do it because she was so big, plus, I didn't want to get her pregnant anyways because she told me if she got pregnant, she could die from diabetes, so I didn't want to get her pregnant and I didn't want to take the risk of having another child with birth defects. I jumped off the bed and put my pants back on. Danielle said, "Too bad you threw your pants on so fast, I would have given you a blow job."

I ran into Danielle C. a couple of years later as I was leaving an AA meeting and took her new number.

Throughout my relationship with Danielle, my therapist was saying to me that I had to accept the way she was and accept the fact that she couldn't reciprocate. He said that you can't fix her.

I heard she ended up homeless, living in a hotel. She was there for a few months and recently told me that she got an apartment in Waltham. She's just spinning her wheels. I did everything for her. I tried to get her a part time job in the cosmetics department at CVS or Walgreens; she couldn't cut it, though. I also, took her to one of the cosmetic stores to apply for a job.

Last I heard she was getting Edinburgh, a social service agency, to pay for her to go to beauty school to become a cosmetologist or hair dresser I asked her whether she thought she could stand up on her feet for eight hours and she said, "Oh yeah I can do it." She used to go to bed at 8:30 pm every night for a forty-six-year-old woman and I didn't got to bed until 11 or twelve in the night; sometimes earlier or later.

One time I bought tickets to see a comedy show that Jimmy Tingle was putting on as a reunion from the Comedy Connection. At the 45th reunion they had about twenty comedians and they were unbelievably funny. She went to bed at 8:30 p.m. The thing didn't start till 10:00 p.m., so she slept all through it. When I got in bed, she ended up on the couch because there wasn't enough room in my bed. It was a double bed and she fell on the floor. She's a big girl. Her friends in Arlington dissuaded her about me. They kept telling her that I was just using her for sex.

One night, when I was home, the police came and gave me a restraining order. It said I could appear in court to tell my part. She claimed in the restraining order that I threatened to cut out her liver and eat it and that I had a knife in my car. The order said that I could go to court and tell my part. I didn't go to court because I was working that day. I just blew it off. I thought nothing would happen. I thought she'd drop it. I thought it was a three-month restraining order, so I called her after three months and evidently she called the police and told them that I had tried to contact her. I got a call from the police. Evidently she had gotten a year's restraining order on me. My friend Fran T. said that she probably got that stuff in her head from watching the crime solving programs that she did…. I heard she ended up homeless, living in a hotel.

I got a call from the Waltham police. The police said that they had neglected to give me a copy of the restraining order.

They said it was their fault and that I should come down to the police station to get a copy of it, not to worry about it, you're not in trouble. Just come by and get a copy of the restraining order. It said I couldn't see her for another full year. The policeman that gave me the restraining order, told me that even if I called her they would arrest me. She had it written into the restraining order that I couldn't see her at the clubhouse that she went to, couldn't see her at her apartment in Waltham. I couldn't contact her on social media. She's got it closed up pretty well. So that's where it stands now.

As I stated, Linda K. and I have gone out a few times. She's very critical about things and I didn't understand it until I read up about her on the internet. I noticed that she had a lot of clinical positions and she told me she'd worked in the Peace Corps and she'd done some other work. She had two or three clinical positions so that's why she was so clinical.

She told me that she was depressed and I understood that, that's why she didn't pick up the papers on her apartment floor. There were scattered papers all around the floor. I said to her, "You have to over-look some things" and she agreed. We went out for coffee one day. We also went to a comedy show, but I was so tired from doing Door-Dash all over the place that I slept through the first part of it.

I had gotten this flyer about a party, but they wouldn't let us in because it was only for people with mental health issues, so we went to this little Paris café in Coolidge Corner and we got crepes and they were pretty good and she was happy about it.

We went to the Senior Center in Needham to see the movie, "Some Like It Hot." It was a pretty good movie. I went to the thrift shop in the Needham Senior Center. I bought a couple of things cheap. We have tea once in a while in my apartment. She comes down for forty-five minutes and leaves. She doesn't have much to say. I usually carry on the conversation. She's very critical. She doesn't like my driving because I cut cars off. I asked her to go to a Friday night dance at the American Legion Post in Bedford. She said, "Yes, okay but I don't dance. I said well we can just listen to the music and watch. Later on she called me and said, "I decided that I don't want to go." I thought it was because she doesn't like to dance, but later she told me that she was afraid of my driving and didn't feel safe with me driving. I said okay from now on I'll drive safely when you're in the car. She really gets a little sensitive about my driving.

Some of My Psychiatric History

When I went inpatient at Newton-Wellesley, I thought it was a riot that I was in the hospital and had a lot of fun there. I told them I was seeing pink elephants and they actually believed me. I was just telling them crazy stuff. Well, anyways I was diagnosed as schizophrenic, and they gave me the antipsychotic Thorazine. I asked him if I could use the hospital library because I didn't think I had schizophrenia at all. I thought I had third stage syphilis. I went to the hospital library to research the symptoms of tertiary-stage syphilis and it turned out the symptoms were the same as schizophrenia. But the doctor said no, it was schizophrenia.

At that time the psychiatrists did the psychotherapy. The aides would talk to you just to keep you grounded. I was in the inpatient unit for about four months. I can't remember now, and then they sent me to the day hospital, their outpatient unit. I was so depressed I didn't want to live. I stayed depressed for about a year. I was bouncing from the inpatient unit to the outpatient unit. They had this Psycho Drama therapy they would do. I wasn't very good at it and I didn't enjoy it at all. I just wanted to get out of there after about a year of bouncing back and forth. I just decided I wanted to live again and start all over. I had to get into a halfway house in order to get out of the hospital. One of the other patients lined up a halfway house for himself, and he said that I could have his slot if I wanted it. So I called them and I made an appointment to visit. I filled out an application.

It was called The Life Center on Bracket Street in Brighton Center. I got accepted and lived there for a bit. I made some good friends there, most of them came from McLean's hospital and McLean's tends to drag out the treatment, kind of institutionalizing them. We enjoyed each other's company. There was a house mother and a house father. There was also an assistant that came like once a week at night. He was working on a degree at Boston University and had been working on it for about seven years. In comparison to me, who got two degrees in five years, he was really working slowly, but he was learning the material. He was a cool dude. There was a bar in Brighton Center near Oak Square that we could go to for a drink.

The house management were pretty liberal. The owner of the halfway house was a guy named Robert R., kind of a funny name, but he would come once a week and we would have a group meeting in the living room. He would talk to everybody about how they were doing. He had a grant from the Department of Mental Health to operate the halfway house. It was very expensive. The rent was like $700 a month and I shared a room with two other people. It was a money-making machine for Robert R. One of the housemates, Bob A. had been going to Cornell and got psychotic and he wanted to kill his mother. He decided to have some experimental surgery done on himself. They drilled a hole in his skull and burned out some section of his brain that caused him to be aggressive.

He was kind of tame as a lamb. He had been studying physics at Cornell and I asked him if he wanted to go back and finish studying physics. He said, "No, I have no interest in it." He was just so passive and had no motivational drive left. I saw him many years later and he seemed to be enjoying the company of a lady friend at a restaurant. He had to go for electroconvulsive treatments (ECT) like once or twice a week he would come back and say, "My spirits are lifted now and then a few days later he'd be down to the dumps again and have to go back in for more ECT treatments. I was afraid they were going to fry his brain. He told me that there were police officers that went in before work and had ECT treatment, then just left and went back to work.

I got a job at Goodwill Industries doing assembly contract work. My psychiatrist who I saw weekly at his office in Newton Center was the same Dr. Stephen H. that I had when I was in the hospital. I had Travelers Insurance from Shell Oil Company. It was one of the best insurances that you can possibly have. I had an inquiry from my section leader at Shell, a nice Italian guy who asked me if I wanted to take disability. They would back date it for me so that I could get some disability if I wanted. I refused because I thought that if I took disability that I may never go back to work. My father had had malaria a couple of times during the war when he was in Africa and he had been wounded once.

Once you get Malaria, it can come back again and they offered him disability, but he didn't take it. Like father, like son. I wanted to work my way back slowly. Dr. Stephen H. stayed with me throughout. When I ended up at Bournewood, he would visit me once or twice a week in the closed-door unit. Finally after there, I went to work at the cleaners. After I had been working there for a couple of years, the insurance company said that they were going to cancel my insurance and stop paying my health bills, because I was no longer an employee of Shell Oil Company and I had a job. I believe that was when Dr. H. and I parted ways.

I went to Dr. Penelope A., the first female psychiatrist in the United States. By then they had deduced that if people with manic depression went untreated they would become psychotic, but it would look like schizophrenia. That's what she claimed had happened to me. So she put me on lithium a bipolar medication. I told her that I'd try it during the day when I'm awake to see what it does. I tried lithium and it shut down all my sensory systems. I wasn't happy. I told her I wasn't going to take it. Since then, I've lost two or three friends due to lithium. If you don't drink a gallon of water a day, the kidneys are adversely affected and you can end up with renal failure. So, she put me on Depakote, which was supposed to help treat the bipolar disorder.

After I left Dr. H., I went to see a PsyD. named Alan A. This was right around the time that Keith was born and he was having problems and they said that a parent had to go home with him. Alan wanted me to have Keith institutionalized. He thought that it was wasteful that I try to recover him.

So, I moved from Alan A. a PsyD. to Richard M., a PhD psychologist who specializes in analysis. I saw Dr. B. a PhD in psychology and a MD in psychiatry. He wanted me to be analyzed eventually by another doctor as a consultant. I went to., the former director of a hospital in Norwood. He analyzed me for like twelve hours (four) three-hour sessions and thought in addition to bipolar, I might have a schizo-affective disorder, but he wasn't sure. Dr. B. asked me what I thought about his report after I had read it and I said well maybe, I don't know.

Sometimes my thoughts break off and get fragmented so maybe I do suffer from a little schizo-affective disorder. Well Dr. B. didn't want to go through the insurance company. He wanted me to pay him out of my pocket $50 a session and then have me bill the insurance company so that was fine with me. Fifty dollars wasn't that much and I got it back. I saw Dick for about six years and Dr. B. about the same amount of time. Then I'd had it with the psychiatric people. The people doing the therapy now were people that are licensed clinical social workers, and I got this guy named Tracy B. to do my therapy. I was with him for a couple years. He was within walking distance from my apartment and it seemed convenient. He was kind of a hard-ball person and I grew to dislike him after a while. So, I looked around for another therapist and someone recommended that I go to Riverside Outpatient Mental Health Clinic and find a therapist there.

So I hooked up with a therapist by the name of Mark N. I've been with him about four years now and he seems to meet my needs. I just make a list of my things that are going on each week and I go over them with him and he has suggestions when I run into obstacles. He'd stayed with me throughout the discourse of Danielle's antics; yes, so I've been through the wringer. washed, dried, and hung up.

My Extended Family at Elliot House

Elliott House is a clubhouse for people who have had mental health issues and through psycho-therapeutic interactive working, it helps people get back out into the community again either through employment or furthering their education. It has two basic units: the Food and Events unit and the Administrative Unit. In the Food and Events unit, you'll find an industrial kitchen with an industrial dishwasher. In the morning there's a meeting for the entire clubhouse staff and members. If necessary, introductions are done, an icebreaker question, such as what's your favorite thing to do in the winter and everybody responds with their favorite thing. The clubhouse is an Internationally Certified Clubhouse. That allows it to be more valuable in the eyes of the Department of Mental Health. They get more funding because of it. The standards are about two pages long and every three years they have to get recertified. So, the standard for the day is read. It's announced who's going to be out of the clubhouse in terms of staff. It's announced if there are going to be tours or new visitors for the day, for potentially new members and then everyone says good morning to each other and have a great day.

Then people retreat back to whatever unit they want to work in for the day. Each unit has a task board. It's a computerized white screen hooked up to a computer where all the tasks for the morning are listed and people volunteer for various tasks throughout the unit. In the morning, sanitizing is an important aspect of the tasks. These are usually done first. Especially in light of the COVID pandemic. Howie L. usually signs up for dishwashing. A couple of people also sign up for making the salad for the day, cutting up vegetables and putting them into a large container. When she's present, Robin is another coordinator of the food and events unit and participates in the food preparation. If there are still not enough staff in the kitchen, the assistant director Zach. Will help out in the kitchen. Steve F., a member likes to operate the Parrot. The Parrot is a little snack bar with coffee and snacks. He has to handle money, sign in and out, and make a deposit if necessary at the end of his shift.

A new member, Mike, likes to help out in the Parrot also. Actually, he does a little bit of everything. He has Asperger's Syndrome and is a little awkward, but he does fine for himself. Valerie S. also likes to do the Parrot, serve the meals, and sometimes sell the tickets for lunch. Ruth G., when she comes in from working at the library or on her day off will do the reception area. She likes to be the receptionist. When she's not there, sometimes Mike does it; he seems to enjoy that, also. Jessica F., Steve's girlfriend and Scotty like to hang out and just converse. Scotty was in a motorcycle accident at about 100 plus miles an hour and hit a guardrail and was in a coma for three months. He waddles a little when he walks because of it. I think his articulation is improving all the time. He talks a lot with Jessica. He spends a lot of time with Jessica, Steve's girlfriend.

Leanne comes in and she doesn't do much of anything. Scotty and Jessica and Leanne became close friends and they just socialize. Liz D., who has seizures and panic attacks all the time likes to be in the conference room by herself with her championship ice skater photographs. She's gotten photographs of them and attached them to cardboard with some plastic wrap and that way she doesn't have any panic attacks and she doesn't have any seizures. Joe C. who works in the kitchen, sometimes when he comes in likes to smoke.

Scotty and Jessica and Leanne like to talk about other people they don't like. For example, Robin the staff member. She's a little bossy and doesn't know what she's talking about sometimes. For example, the other day, I put the coffeepot through the washing machine and went to take it out and give it to the fellow at the Parrot, so he could make coffee and Robin said, "You have to wear gloves," and she goes and reaches in there to get the coffeepot.

So I said to her, "I'm going to give it to a guy who is not wearing any gloves and he's going to make the coffee." I should have said no, it's illogical what you are saying, but anyways I did what she said because I didn't want to be ruffling her feathers too much. The next time I'm going to let her have it because she's not really that smart. Pretty much, maybe I'll take out the trash that's about it. There's Steve F., he knows everything about sports—basketball, baseball, football, and hockey. He's an expert on sports and he likes one particular radio station and always tells people to listen to it. Fran T. comes in and does as he pleases. I've known Fran since 1981. 31 years. Sandy, the fellow I lived with, had taken me to Second Story and Fran used to go there too. Fran, was an anti-vaxxer for many, many months and he recently got his first vaccination. He said, "Well, I don't want to die." That's what most people who take the vaccine say to themselves. I don't want to die, I want to live.

The Food and Events unit always helps plan the food aspect for events that we are going to have such as the Thanksgiving luncheon and annual barbecue fundraiser. We have a Halloween party and a St. Patrick's Day event and a winter celebration around Christmas and Chanukah.

The other unit is the Admin Unit, which I'm more familiar with. Although I did get a job as a dishwasher for a year at the Fessenden school, a private boys school. After about a year I had it with the job. My boss wanted me to sweep and mop what amounted to about a half of a football field worth of area and I was unhappy. I asked the boss for a raise and he said all we give out raises in September. I said, "Oh no, I got my raise last April. He said well we give all our raises out in September. I said well you increased my responsibilities you have to increase my pay. He said either take it or leave it, so the next day I called and spoke with the employment coordinator at Elliot House who was supposed to support me and he just shrugged his shoulders and didn't know what to do, so that day I called and said I'm leaving it. That put them in a bind for about two or three months.

I also got a job in food processing at the JCC (Jewish Community Center) for about three or four months. My boss was this guy David N. He had a contract for the indoor café and the outdoor café during the summer by the pool. He promised me that he would give me a college kid to work with me when they opened by the pool. He re-neged on it and gave me a guy for about an hour per day. Once the outdoor café was open, I got burned out providing all the food for the indoor café and then all the food for the outdoor café. So I ended up in the hospital as usual.

So the industrial kitchen at Elliot was going to serve a purpose. Members can learn to be a dishwasher or a food processor, like I did. So now I stay away from the kitchen and just work in the Admin-istrative Unit mostly. We have a weekly newsletter that we publish, telling all about the events around the clubhouse and what's going on at the clubhouse and identifying people's birthdays for that week and of the celebrations that are going on and we put out flyers for special events, plan trips, and we recently opened the Studio 255 shop. I did most of the paperwork for the thrift shop to open. Every day the Admin Unit inputs all the statistics for the clubhouse's members in the Salesforce database that they are using now. We input all the at-tendance and all of the contacts between members and staff whether it be by phone or in person. That way all the data is put together and sent to the Department of Mental Health, which pays for the services the clubhouse provides to the members based on the data.

Members can't be paid for anything they do at the clubhouse in accordance with the International Clubhouse Standards. In the Admin Unit, in addition to the statistics, we make greeting cards for people whether it be sympathy, thank you, birthday, get well, etc. Everybody gets a free meal ticket on their birthday month. The Admin Unit makes flyers for holidays and social events. They help people find jobs or go back to school. They help people with housing.

Steve C. is the new director and he's been there for about six months now. Allison S was the former director. She had been there for over six years and when she had a second child, she decided to stay home with her two children. She was a wonderful person. Everybody loved her. The only thing that was kind of cold was that she said to me, "You know, Keith will never be able to come here." I thought that was rather cold of her. She told me once that her father was an alcoholic and that he was a director of a group residence program. The staff members in the Admin Unit now are Donna N., the Unit and Education Coordinator whose been there for about five or six years. Emma left about six months ago after having been there about 1½ years. Emmie, a Unit and Employment Coordinator whose a dynamo has been there about 9 months now.

They haven't been able to hire a second Employment Coordinator to fill Zach's position. Zach moved up to Assistant Director when Steve moved to Director. Zach and Steve used to be inseparable. They went to college together, were roommates there and then Steve got Zach a job at Elliot House, and then when Allison left, Steve got the job as Director and then Zack as Assistant Director. Steve started out in the kitchen and worked hard. He has a second job working in a liquor store. He's a hard-working guy. I'm waiting for him to get me a job at Adelson.

I spoke to him today and he said it looks pretty good that they're going to have a TE position open there. The usual members in the Admin Unit are Mary P. She loves to make cards by hand and send out the Weekly Newsletter. She's a little slow on the computer, so Donna has to give her orders all the time on how to do this and how to do that. Donna was getting a little bossy with me and I told her not to do it, because I already know how to do it and I don't need to be ordered around. She agreed and said, "Yeah you're right. I was just so used to treating these other people that don't have the computer skills that you have this way. I've been treating everybody that way." So we just left it at that with a mutual understanding. Tom Button, who loves to enter the statistics., Bob B., who loves to write "How-to Procedures" for everything in the Admin Unit. He used to be a technical writer. Kathy S. likes to work on Wednesdays to do the menu with Mary P.

When we're going to have an event, I do outreach quite often; I make up a script based upon the event and I usually call maybe a hundred or more people to see if they want to attend. I have spreadsheets and I add columns to it so that I can get all of the categories that need to be addressed.

I was socializing with people outside the clubhouse in the smoking area and I kept saying that I haven't smoked in over thirty years and after a couple of weeks of that, I went over to one of the fellows and asked if I could buy two cigarettes for a dollar and ever since then I've been up and running with cigarettes three months off, three months on, a month-and-a-half off, a month on; it's a hard habit to break once you've started. I've gone to nicotine anonymous. In-person meetings before that pandemic. Also, the conference calls.

So now I'm broke. I have no job. I was doing DoorDash, and you make like $11 an hour comes down to about $9 an hour after fuel and maintenance, below minimum wage. There was a class action suit against them about that and I didn't want to get involved with it because I didn't want to get my partner pissed off.

Between stopping smoking cigarettes and driving for DoorDash, I just can't make ends meet, so I'm probably now going to have to sell my Toyota Corolla. The reason I can't use my Toyota Corolla for Uber, which pays better than DoorDash, is that the front seat upholstery is stained, plus the trunk is full and when you do Uber, they want the trunk to be empty and you're upholstery to be clean.

My Visit to Fountain House

A couple of years ago I visited Fountain House in New York City. It was the original International Clubhouse. Some people who had been in a psychiatric unit in New York decided to meet every day outside the hospital to give each other support; eventually it got so big they hired staff to work there.

Fountain House has some rooms that you can stay in while visiting. They have a kitchen and a whole dining area. What I liked about Fountain House most was that it had a memoriam section in this memorial book that remembers members who had passed, and they would have pictures and a little caption about the person. I didn't like climbing the ninety steps up to my room, though.

My Artwork at the Senior Center

The Newton Senior Center has an open studio art class that is facilitated by David W. He had been a professional portrait artist for seven years and he's been in art for twenty-five-plus years. I wanted to do a portrait of my son in pastel. It took me about eighteen hours to complete. David put the finishing touch on the eyes. He got a Q-tip dipped in white and dipped it on the eye so it made a pupil. When a copy of it was sent to my ex-wife's sister, she looked at it and said, "Keith has eyes just like the family." David never even looked at the picture when he did the eyes. I had to put it in my storage. I hope to frame it someday. I had wanted to do a polo match drawing ever since the days when I knew Joseph Santoro; the second-best watercolor artist on the globe. I went to his gallery once in Rockport and he had a beautiful polo match. I asked him how much he wanted and he said about $5,000. It was way out of my reach. So, I asked David if I paid him, like, fifteen to thirty bucks per hour if he'd help me do a polo match. I had a nice photograph of one, so we cut out only two horses with their riders and their polo sticks.

David did most of the drawing of the horses and then I did the background for it. It only cost me about sixty bucks so we got a beautiful portrait. When I was in New York visiting Fountain House, I went to the Metropolitan Museum of Art to seek out the Rembrandts and the other impressionists and they weren't anywhere as good as David's horses were. He even had the hoof kicking up the dirt. He showed the sinews of the horses' muscles. When I got back, I told David that Rembrandt's horses weren't as good as his. I said maybe we should donate the Polo Match to a museum. His response was that it won't be worth anything until after "you and I are dead." I have it in my storage unit along with the portrait of Keith. I have some other miscellaneous acrylic drawings that I've done there also.

One of the other artists at the open studio, Margo V., told me that it would help me a lot if I took a drawing course. So I applied to take a drawing course. The fellow giving the course was a watercolor artist, but he taught basic drawing. Every week he would have another still life set up on the tables for about seven weeks.

We would begin our drawings in the classroom and then we would take them home and complete them during the week before the next class. He would show them at the class and there would be a class critique on each one of them. He asked me where I learned to draw. I told him that my mother had taught me how to draw when I was little. I guess I was pretty good at it. Elliot House displayed my drawings on the Art Bulletin Board for about a month.

Well, I forgot to call my son today. I usually call every day around 7:30 p.m., and we speak. I usually say, "Hi, Keith, Daddy here, I love you, honey, Daddy here. I love you, honey." Then I ask him, "How you doing?" He usually says, "Good;" then I say, "I'm happy to hear you're doing good. I'm smiling." Then, I say, "Okay, I'm going to blow you a kiss," and I take my hand, kiss it with my lips and blow the kiss through the phone and he goes "Mwah" back to me. I ask if you are in the living room or the bedroom and he tells me where he is, so if he's in his bedroom, which he is the majority of the time by 7:30. So, I'll say, "Have a good night, sleep tight, don't let the bedbugs bite; night, night," and that's about it and I say, "Please give the phone back to whoever it was who answered the phone and he gives it back. He has a lot of receptive language. His expressiveness is very, very low. Maybe "music." "Tape" maybe three to six other words expressively he had 125 before at seven years old before they took away our home program. And he had about 250 receptive words before. Plus, he had some full sentences.

My other extended family members are Paul W. who has been a close friend for over sixteen years, is an audiophile and a great chess player. He and I go out for dinner once in a while, and I try to split the bill. He has a large-screen TV and a fireplace in his apartment. It's quite cozy. Unfortunately this past year, he has been on dialysis three times a week, and it kills most of his days, but it doesn't seem to bother him, because he kind of likes to sit in his captain's chair all day anyways watching TV and listening to music. Some of the other neighbors were Elana, Shirley, and Carol. Brian is a friend of mine, who lived above me and I took him out quite often for coffee and dessert snacks. I've taken him to restaurants and treated him. He doesn't understand the idea of reciprocity and I got kind of tired of treating him all the time, so I haven't contacted him for several weeks, since I've been broke. He has money to buy coffee and desserts for himself. What a taker he is.

He's got a homemaker who comes every day of the week, a social worker who takes him shopping and to doctor visits for him and his cat "Tiger." He bought me a $10 gift card once or twice in the fifteen years that I've been treating him. I've spent hundreds of dollars on him. I called him a couple of weeks ago and asked him if he wanted to go out, but he'd have to pay for himself, but as usual he said that he didn't have any money, that he was broke. I got a call from his sister saying "why are you hassling my brother? You used to be best friends with him." I have to call her to tell her that I treated him all the time. He doesn't pay for anything and he just expects everything for free.

One of my other friends is Debbie G. and she told me she was gay, that she had been married to a woman, but she told me that she likes both men and women. We hung around for about a year or two. She is blind in one eye and walks with one of those feelers. We go out to restaurants. She pays for herself and I pay for the tip because she never comes up with money for the tip. On my seventieth birthday, I expected at least a card from her. I didn't expect anything else. When I confronted her, she got mad and she said only babies ask for gifts. I said, "I didn't ask you for a gift. I asked for a card." So, we got into a big fight and one thing led to another and we weren't talking to each other anymore.

I finally decided to put the make on Debbie. We were sitting on her couch next to each other and I asked her if I could kiss her; she said okay. She wouldn't french kiss with me, so I knew something wasn't quite right. I asked her if we could make love and she replied, "It's sex just sex." And she got very angry at me and told me that she likes women. After that, she tried to befriend me again because she knew I had the car and I was taking her places and she was enjoying it; now, she didn't have that luxury, so I knew she would lose out in the end. Debbie is very intelligent.

We had an RSC (residential service coordinator) named Pam M. for the almost sixteen years that I had been living at New Falls Apartment. I believe that Pam had worked there over twenty years.

Emily F., the Property Manager at New Falls Apartments, (the most recent one), gave Pam a bad review. Pam had been there for over twenty years, as I noted. We'd been through at least four Property Managers, since I'd been there and Pam was literally crying on my shoulder, about it. She didn't know what to do. She wrote a nasty letter to Emily and left it on her desk. I told her not to burn her bridges behind her. "You've been here twenty years," I said. "You've been a good employee and you've done really well by the tenants, so don't burn your bridges behind you." So, she decided to go to the Human Resource Department for Barkan Management, the property management company. The human resource person there told her to calm down and told her to wait a couple of weeks and give her notice and just to move on and not burn her bridges behind her; like I told her. So, she went back to Emily's office and took back the nasty letter she'd written. She decided that she was not signing off on her review by Emily agreeing with it, just signing and acknowledging that she had read it.

Emily was after me. It was wintertime. I was working at the auto auction. One day during the cold of winter, I recall that I had two pairs of pants and two shirts on. Maybe once per year, I'd run out of underwear; so I might not have had underwear on. Later, when I got back to my apartment, I was doing some work on the computer and I needed something from my car and that's when I ran up to my car. It just took me a few seconds. I ran up to my car to retrieve something. The stairs were in front of my apartment and my car was parked at the top of the stairs.

My pants must had fallen down below my hips and evidently one of the kids in the neighborhood saw me as he was walking by and went home and told his mother. So, the boy's mother, Shelby R. called the police. I had been out working at the Auto Auction since 4:00 a.m. in the morning. I was exhausted from the auction that day and the temperature had been below freezing. It was currently around 6:30 p.m.

All of a sudden, I get a ring at my doorbell. I went into the hallway and there was a male cop and a female cop. The male cop asked me if I had recently been out on the sidewalk with my pants down. I said,

"No, I don't know what you're talking about." I told them that when I got home from work, I had visited Pam in the community room and she had some good news. She had found an RSC position in the Wellesley Housing Authority. Pam told me that she had been trying to call Paul to let him know, but she didn't want me to tell anyone else. She wanted Emily to think that she was going to be out in the street. She asked me if I could tell Paul. So, I went to Paul's apartment to tell him that Pam had found another job. He was just a building away from my apartment.

The police officer said that he was going to talk to the tenant again to see what he had to say.

About fifteen minutes later, they came back with a sergeant, and the sergeant told me that they spoke to the boy again and he's very articulate and he claims that he saw me with my pants down. So, again I told him that I didn't know what he was talking about. I had forgotten that I even had run up the stairs. It was seconds out of a very long busy day. Maybe my pants were falling down for a few seconds, when I ran up the stairs. So, he said, "Okay I'll go talk to the boy again and maybe I'll come back or maybe not. About twenty minutes later, I got a phone call from the sergeant asking me to come into the hall. He had come back and he said I talked to the boy who is very articulate and he described you and used your name. By then, I was very upset.

The sergeant told me that he was going to charge me with "Open and Gross Lewdness and Lascivious Behavior." The sergeant said that it was a serious charge. I told him that I'd never heard of it. He said that I should google it and get a lawyer. Then he told me, I have two options, "one is to either arrest you and bring you to jail now or two issue you a summons for a hearing." So I was shocked. I said those are my two options. He said, "No, those are my two options." So, I said, "Send me a summons to appear in court."

I googled it and found out that it was a felony and if the person was stunned and shocked by it even though there were no other witnesses, I could be held liable. However, the law states that it has to be an intentional act and certainly this had been an accident. It had been no more than a wardrobe malfunction.

So, I called Atty. Steven A. he had done bankruptcy for me and he said that he wanted about $25,000 for him to represent me upfront. And I said I don't have that kind of money so I hunted and hunted and I think that I used something like 800-411-Laws and got in touch with this lawyer named Atty. Stephen R. eventually, and he said that he could do it for $300 per hour so I agreed.

At the hearing, there was a magistrate and a court stenographer typing out the proceedings. The sixteen-year-old, Quentin, and his mother Shelby R. My ex-wife Janice A. came to give me support. I had only seen the boy a few times the entire time fifteen to sixteen years that I lived at New Falls Apartments. Once or twice at a birthday party, once when he came to play Bingo with the seniors, and once at the food pantry where I volunteered and also just in passing in the parking lot.

The magistrate's name was his Honor S. So, the judge asked the boy to tell what happened.

So, Quentin told him that it was about 6:30 p.m., he was coming home from work and he heard a car door close and when he looked over he saw me with my pants down and my stomach and testicles showing. Then he ran home, told his mother and she called the police.

The judge asked him how he knew my first name, and the boy said, "Well, I volunteered once, at the food pantry and Larry was there volunteering too." The boy alleged that I had looked at some girls walking by, when he got home from school weirdly and that I was driving around the bus stop a couple of times. It was probably because I had forgotten my wallet or phone and had to drive around the block again to get my wallet before going to work. So the judge asked my lawyer if I wanted to say anything and my lawyer said no because anything I said might be held against me in a court trial.

So eventually the judge after listening to all the evidence said that there were no grounds for the charge and he was dropping it. My lawyer told the judge that he had recommended that I move. The judge said, "That would probably be a good idea since there would probably be animosity between myself and the other party."

The Property Manager took me to the Housing Court via their lawyer Atty. T. My lawyer met with the property manager's lawyer and they came up with five steps that I had to comply with, including moving within three months. I told my lawyer that I had not done anything wrong and that the charge had been dropped and he said, "Larry, you're stuck in the weeds." The Property Manager's lawyer told my lawyer that Shelby and Quentin were in the building and if I didn't sign the agreement that they'd bring them up to testify. My lawyer said that I should sign the agreement to move. My ex-wife was with me also.

He told me that I didn't have the money to defend myself in court and that it was going to cost me thousands of dollars to do so. So, I signed the agreement. In hindsight my ex and I agree that we should have fired my lawyer on the spot and gotten a public defender to help me out.

In the meantime, I'd spoken to somebody they said to contact at the Middlesex Legal Association. I spoke with this fellow named Atty.

Joseph S. After I explained the situation, he told me that it was too bad that I hadn't contacted him first because none of what transpired would have happened. He also knew Barkan's lawyer and said that he was known to be a cutthroat lawyer. He said to send him all the documents and he'd looked into it. So, I put together a whole package of all the documents. There were about one hundred pages they'd have to review. I called him two weeks later and he said that he didn't have a chance to look at it. I called him two weeks later again and he said he still hadn't had a chance to look at it. Then finally, he said he was moving and then he was going on vacation and after that he'd looked at it. What a JERK.

Well, I was working with a mental health case manager from DMH., Reggie A. and after a couple of months of working with him. He told me that he'd only been with DMH a couple of years. I said to myself that he didn't have any contacts to work with. In the meantime, I had applied to about fourteen different places. The Newton Housing Authority had a person who said okay we have a place for you at the Hamilton Grove. And then when it came time for me to look at the apartment that was available, she told me that the lease manager said that the apartments were all taken. I went to another person that had an apartment available in the Nonantum area. She was the property manager. She told me that I had first dibs on it. She showed it to me. Then she turned me down because of the documents in the housing court. She told me that if I got turned down the first time, I could appeal and usually the appeals won.

So, I appealed to the assistant property manager and after spending hours with her on the phone, I got a letter from her saying that my appeal was denied. I got in touch with Ruthanne F., the mayor of Newton, and she had one of her flunkies look into it for me to see if they could find me a place. I got a call a couple of days later that they had a place for me, which would be shared with twelve other housemates. I couldn't even imagine sharing a kitchen with twelve other people. I had this guy from DMH Reggie working with me. He had spoken to my property owner, Emily F. about the rent issue that had transpired and it was resolved.

Reggie finally came up with a contact at the Golda Meir House, in Auburndale (another village of Newton) and I had applied there and there was a five-year waiting list. Reggie said he could get me in if I wanted to. I told him that my parents didn't like it there. They regretted moving there and I remember my mother complaining about all the construction work that was going on when she lived there. She hated the noise. A fellow that was one of my neighbors at New Falls worked at the Golda Meir House at the desk and he told me they had remodeled the whole place and it's gorgeous and he'd love to live there and eventually have his mother live there in the future. So, I ended up in the hospital from fatigue at trying to find a place to live after about four or five months, head-on looking and looking, searching and searching, and being turned down and being turned down and being turned down.

Reggie called me at the hospital and asked me when I was getting out, so that I could look at the apartment. I told him about two or three days. So we set up a date of about two or three days away, so I could get out and look at the apartment. Myra M., the Director was there and the Occupancy Specialist, Geoffrey Y. The apartment was very nice. It was at ground level and had an open kitchen that I liked. The only thing I didn't like was the long corridor that I had to walk down to get to it. When we went back upstairs, I asked Myra if there was underground parking or not and she said "we don't have any space for your car."

She looked at Reggie and said, "Can't he use New Mo or the Ride?"

So I said to her, "No, I don't qualify for either one of those." Then. I said, "Would you like to be told that you can't drive anymore?" That you had to give up your car. I told Myra that my parents had a car when they lived there. So, the next day I spoke with Pam and told her about it and she told me to ask him if they can make a "reasonable accommodation for my car." So, I called Reggie and I told him what she had said. He said, "Well, let me get back to Myra and talk to her about it. The next day he got back to me and said that they had found a parking spot for me.

My Life at the Golda Meir House

So I moved to the Golda Meir House in December of last year. I've been here a little over one year. I organized everything very nicely to move. I got moving boxes and arranged for a mover. I color-coded all the boxes with stickers. Red sticker meant kitchen, blue meant bedroom, yellow meant kitchen or bathroom (however, it was labeled) green meant living room. I felt like I was deserted on a beach. So, I spoke with the social worker here. If they knew anyone that could help me organize a little. They recommended the Moving Mavens. I called the Moving Mavens and they charged $90 an hour. And they had a minimum of four hours. So I hired her, but they came out with one of the gals and after two hours I was exhausted.

She'd help me a bit by organizing it. Hang some pictures on the walls. I told her that I needed something for the bathroom to hold all my toiletries and she said she would look into it for me at Bed, Bath, and Beyond and I also told her that I needed a paper towel rack for the kitchen. So, she said she would look into it for me. I got an email from her with a recommendation from Bed, Bath, and Beyond for a couple of toiletry cabinets and a couple of different paper toilet holders for the kitchen. So I purchased one of the toiletries holder carts and I got one of the towel racks that she had shared with me. I felt a little bit better by then.

The Residential Service Coordinator (RSC) buddied me up with Leslie P. to give me a tour of the place and answer any questions that I had. It was a three-month commitment for her and she said that I could call her any time after 10:00 a.m. until about 7:00 p.m. Leslie knows a lot of people. So every time I had a question, I would call Leslie for about three months. After I was here for a while, Marina, the ambassador at the front desk came over to me and said, "I'm almost afraid to ask you, but do you think you could volunteer to work at the desk a couple of days a week for three or four hours?" I said, "Yes, I could do that." So I volunteered at the desk and Marina couldn't do any small talk. She was always busy except when the upper executives came from the board to visit. She sucks up to them big time.

Marina always had criticism. No matter what I did, she would find something wrong. I would just say, "Okay."

Then I got a paid job working for Vinfen as an outreach worker. Laura B. was my supervisor. She was the director and she worked out of a group home in Needham, Massachusetts. Her office was in the basement of the house and I went through all the training in order to get employed. You have to have a physical check, credit check, CORI check, and a fingerprint check. I had to take a Red Cross course to get certified in CPR and Red Cross. I participated in all the training; it took hours and hours. You have to put your own driving info into the database. Also, I had to put my hours into a different database and had to keep daily progress notes on all my clients. It was hard to do.

I had about four or five clients in total. One of them was a black guy. He thought that I was his personal slave, what a jerk. He had gotten shot in the neck. Evidently, someone put a gun to his neck and he turned around and tried to knock the gun out of the guy's hand, but the gun went off and put a bullet in his neck and he was being rehabilitated. He claimed he wanted to open an outdoor restaurant concession stand.

He never even said thank you. He made me wait for hours outside the YMCA after telling me he'd be out in an hour. The last time that I took him to the Y, he had me waiting like two hours beyond what he told me. I had to go into the Y and locate him and drag him out. He got all pissed at me and asked me why I hadn't called him. I told him that I thought that he put his phone in his locker. So, we had it out. One day on the way to taking him for his haircut, he asked me to stop so that he could pick up some over-the-counter pharmaceuticals for his aunt and then take him to his aunt's. When I took him for his haircut, he had me wait in my car for at least an hour. Then, besides taking him to an OT appointment at Spaulding rehab, he had me take him all the way up to Salem, Massachusetts from Roslindale. He had a friend running for city councilor or something and he wanted to go up and show his support. So, I was like his personal chauffeur.

I didn't like it and I told my boss, Laura, but she said, "Why do you care? You're getting paid for it anyway." I was getting paid to be an outreach worker, not a personal slave.

Also, we'd set a time for me to pick him up in Roslindale at his apartment and I'd arrive on time and he wouldn't even be dressed yet. I'd have to wait like an hour in his living room for him to get ready. Finally, I told him that I'd pick him up a half hour before the time we were supposed to leave and he was still late. So, I finally had it out with him at the Y, like I said before. Laura was scheduled to meet with him the next week and we agreed that he and I weren't a good fit and that she'd take over covering for him.

I also asked Laura whether there was a little support group for the outreach workers and she said there wasn't and that she could give me support. It was a little difficult to get in touch with her.

One of my other clients, Joseph F. was a nice guy. He expressed his gratitude to me all the time. He was very big and needed to use a wheelabrator to walk because his legs would give out otherwise. He had Type 1 diabetes. I had to visit him twice a week. I was supposed to remind him to take his glucose level and discuss his staying in contact with his two daughters. He didn't speak to his daughters, but he told me that they texted on a regular basis. I took him to his doctor's appointments, to his diabetes doctor, to his kidney doctor and to his dermatologist. He never let me come in to his appointments, even though Laura told me that I should go in. She told me that she used to go in. But he wouldn't let me, so I just said fine. I wasn't going to argue with him about it.

They wanted me to get him a motorized scooter. I did some research and discovered that a scooter wouldn't be safe for him. He could tip over in it and get hurt. He needed a motorized wheelchair. There was a PT working with him, who had left and she recommended the scooter. I spoke with the new PT working with him and she agreed that he needed a motorized wheelchair. It has six wheels on it because it's very heavy.

Another one of my clients was this guy Chuck M. from Medford, who was living with his mother. He got hit by a car and had some brain damage. The division I worked in was the brain trauma division. His mom, Florence, was older and very concerned about him finding an apartment close to her house to make sure he'd be okay after she passed on. I had to find him a new apartment to go to. I used all my expertise at apartment hunting to help him find a new apartment. After about three weeks, we found an apartment.

He had a couple of motorbikes that he wanted to sell, so I put them on Craigslist for him. Never got any response really.

His mom was really nice, but they got on each other's nerves and she wanted to make sure that he was taken care of and had his own place to live after she passed. She was very nice to me when I came over. She offered to make me a sandwich and I said "Okay." She gave me a sandwich and when I told Laura my boss about it, she said, "Oh you can't take anything to eat from the clients. You can take a drink, but not take anything to eat." So the next couple of times I was asked by his mother if I wanted a sandwich. I said, "No, I have my lunch in the car." Chuck M. and I found a place for him to live. It was only about ½ mile from his mom's house. We had to do a lot of paperwork and Laura screwed up half of the paperwork. She sent an email to the wrong email address.

One of the other clients I had was John E. He was in a wheelchair in a nursing home and wanted to get out of there. He'd been there about two and a half years. Due to gangrene, they cut off his toes and then they cut off his foot and then they cut off his leg.

He had to put money in his Ride account, so I had to take him to the bank to put money into his account. I thought we would just have to go through an ATM machine, but he said he had to get out and go into the bank. I had to fold up his wheelchair and get it in the backseat of my car. I folded it up and it damaged the roof of my car. I was so excited about all this, that I left my briefcase out in the parking lot and didn't realize it. The briefcase had my computer and all my notes, and if I didn't find it, I would probably get fired. I had to stop by my bank on the way. Then we went to his bank. Then it dawned on me that my briefcase was missing. I called my bank because I wanted to see if I had left it there. They said no and I called the nursing home and asked them if anyone had turned in a briefcase and they said no. John E. had been smoking Cigarillos, I was so anxious about the briefcase that I asked him for one a couple of times.

I'd stopped smoking before that. He said to me, just tell them it was stolen. When we got back to the nursing home, my briefcase was standing against the wall at the entrance to the nursing home, so I said, "Oh thank God for that." But I was hooked on cigarettes again.

I got him about seven applications to places he wanted to live. He wanted to live in Revere or about three or four different communities. He needed to have a birth certificate. Most of the applications said he had to have his Social Security Certificate. He told me that the nursing home had stolen all his documentation. So, I applied for a birth certificate. He was born in Los Angeles and they wrote back to me saying that I didn't qualify to receive the birth certificate for him because I was only his social worker. It had to be another family member or whatever; so anyways I was getting more and more stressed.

I dropped the black guy from my client list and Laura assigned me this guy up in Lowell, who had been an engineer, but had had a bad car accident. His car had hydroplaned off the road into a tree. He had been in a coma. He was wheelchair-bound and it was hard to understand what he was saying.

The first week he said that he wanted to go to Bob's Sporting Goods. So, I took him there and he purchased a couple of jerseys for about $50. I had to help him find the correct size. I was pushing his wheelchair around the mall. The next week, I took him to a Mexican restaurant that he wanted to go to. He treated me. When we got home, his sister was there and told me that he couldn't afford to keep spending money like he was. She asked me if there wasn't a place I could take him that didn't cost anything. I said I didn't know, just the park that he liked to visit. She was always around after I brought him home and she was all over me.

I was getting burned out quickly, my nerves were shot and I had very little job support.

So, I spoke with my shrink, Dr. T. and he told me to unload.

One of the guys, this South Korean guy, Jung J., that I smoked with in the designated smoking area handed me a joint one day. He's about seventy-eight years old and he handed me this joint and said, "You smoke now?" and I said, "No, I have to smoke it later off the HUD property." Due to the property being partially HUD (federally funded) you can't smoke pot on the premises. Because it was federal and smoking marijuana was still illegal in the federal government. For Massachusetts it was okay; it was legalized, but the federal government has not yet legalized it. It's up to the states.

I had gotten wicked stoned by the joint that Jung had given me and I still hadn't recovered twenty-six hours later. I called in sick one of the days that I was supposed to be with Joe F., but I had co-ordinated the wheelchair person and his PT person to meet at Joe's and customize the chair for him. They really didn't need me there for that anyway.

I closed the windows in my car and I had half a joint. I was hallucinating and I thought it had cyanide or some other poison in it. I pulled all the cords in my apartment emergency cords and I went out to the hallway and I hit the elevator button. The elevator door opens and says, "Going up." It went up and I thought it was taking me to heaven; it scared me, so I got out of the elevator and pressed the button to 1 and it said, "Going down" and I thought I was going to hell; so I pressed O, which is the floor above me and I said, "I owe, I O off to work I go."

I have to go to work because I have bills to pay. It affected my whole nervous system dramatically. I was shaking like a leaf. When the overnight supervisor came to me, he asked me, "What's the matter?" I said something like I smoked ½ joint that this Asian guy gave me and I think it had poison in it. I need to go to the hospital. He got an ambulance and told them that I'd smoked something and I thought I was poisoned; so I got to the hospital and I didn't even remember getting there from the apartment, but when I got to the hospital they sent me through triage 1. I told the nurse that I thought the joint had cyanide in it and I was going to die. The nurse said that if it was cyanide, I'd be dead in thirty seconds. So, I ruled that out and they evaluated me out in the corridor.

The emergency room put me in a wheelchair after about six and a half hours. It looked like all the people were actors at the hospital. They were just playing a role. They're all actors. I was a little paranoid. I texted. I didn't think I was going to survive, so I wrote all the way in a text message to Debbie G. The next time I saw her she said it sounded like you were writing a script for a movie and I said yeah that's what I was doing, in case I died; it would be a record of it." So finally, I walked out of the emergency room about 10:30 at night. I went out and talked to a girl sitting outside who had brought her son into the hospital. I told her that they had me waiting like two hours in the waiting room. She told me that if you tell them that you're having heart palpitations, they take you right away. She told me about her house that had caught on fire from something someone threw in her yard and how the air conditioner blew through the window and luckily she had gotten property insurance. She got a whole new house in Stoughton after that. And she went back into the hospital. I eventually decided to walk home and blow off the hospital.

It turned out that the Golda Meir people called my sister because she was my emergency contact. I went through Golda Meir House to get the ambulance, so the lady in the emergency room asked me if I wanted to talk to my sister. I said, "Yeah, tell her I'm fine." The next time I spoke to her, she told me she was all upset. She said they told her that I went to the Mass General or something she couldn't make out clearly what the Golda Meir person had said, so she'd called the two psychiatric units in Newton-Wellesley to see if I was there and I wasn't there. My sister was a bit upset. She said, "What do you think you are? You're acting like a teenager; you think you're a teenager. You're just killing brain cells."

The next day, I thought I'd gotten some other kind of poison; that was slow. I googled it on my phone and it said there was a kind of poison that's a slow death. So I started walking to the hospital, but I couldn't make it. I got to the Woodland trolley stop and said to myself, okay I'm going to call an ambulance from here, that way, they won't bother my sister again. So, I dialed 9-1-1.

This time I told him I was right at the entrance to the Woodland T Stop. And the person on the other end of the line told me that she'd stay on the line and wait until they came. I said, "I'll let you know when they get here." The ambulance came and drove past the entrance all the way down to the back of the T Stop. So, I went out and started walking towards the ambulance and I waved them down and said, "Here I am, here I am" so they put me in the ambulance and I asked the ambulance driver about the poison, Strychnine. He said that he had never heard of it, so I told him to google it. I had left my glasses in the apartment so I couldn't read the symptoms.

.So, I told them that I taught them something. I asked the older EMT, had anything ever happened to him like this, and he said, "Yeah, I took some edibles once in my kitchen and I thought the Germans were invading my apartment. They're flying over me and the German soldiers were coming to get me."

I asked how long does a high usually last, so he said he'd heard that like twenty-four hours maximum. This stuff kept me high probably closer to twenty-six to thirty hours.

First they put me through triage number 1 and then they were in the corridor inside the emergency room. I stayed there until about 10:30 p.m., and then they asked me if I felt better and I said yes, so they were going to discharge me and they told me that there'd be a Lyft outside for me. I told the nurse that I only lived a couple of blocks away and could walk, but she said the weather's not good out there right now. So she told me there'd be a black vehicle waiting for me. When I got outside there were three or four black vehicles outside and the weather was fine, so I decided just to walk home. I got a follow-up call from a nurse at the hospital the next day to make sure I was alright. I didn't respond to the call.

I couldn't work the next day, so I called in sick and Debbie G. told me to take the next day off too and I said no, I'm going in. I have to finish this.

I was getting tired of running from Framingham to Lowell and so I finally told my boss that I couldn't do it anymore and that I was handing in my resignation. I said I'll give you one week's resignation notice; she said to me, "Well, we really prefer two weeks' notice," and I sent her resignation letter and told her that I was leaving in one week. My psychiatrist told me to unload everything anyway to Laura, because I was really getting stressed out. The job is killing me for $15 per hour. When I took the job, my boss there told me that it only pays $15 per hour; She said Social Services doesn't pay too much, you know.

The Present

Currently, I'm driving for DoorDash. Last week they had me go anywhere from Roxbury to Somerville and Waltham. It was absurd. It knocked me out for two or three days afterwards. I turned seventy years old in August 2022.

I am waiting to hear about an Office Assistant job at the Adelson family foundation. Steve said they have an easy job; they're going to put it in parallel with the SE job that Jeff C. has. It's like an office boy job, but I think that if I take it, maybe Keith would be able to do it later on. Jeff knows how to milk jobs, that's for sure. He milked Maloney properties for years.

DoorDash is a grind when you open up the app and pick your hours you go to be operative. Usually, I do like six in the morning till two in the afternoon. I can make like $75.00 or so in five plus hours. My ex-wife said to just do delivery of food. She said, What if you drive for Uber and one of your female passengers yells rape?

I went out to Bernardi Toyota to see if I could get a new car. I have about $16,266 left on my car loan. The car is worth about $22,000 in good condition according to Kelley Blue Book. The Toyota dealership would only give me about $14,000 for it. The monthly payments would be over $40 above what I pay now—$306/month. I tried to see if I could purchase a cheaper car like a Hyundai. My monthly payments would be lower than having a brand-new Toyota. I contacted them yesterday and they said that they didn't have any of the lower-priced models yet; hopefully, next week they would have the Venue in. He was going to give me first dibs on one of the lower-priced models. I believe it's called a Venue. They have the Accents and then the next step up is the Venue.

Previously, after two years of hoofing it, I got a Hyundai Accent on Route 2 in Leominster and my monthly payments were about $325. I had fair credit. I had had a bankruptcy, so the loan interest rate was high. The sales manager told me to make sure I paid my first three months payments on time, and then go to a Mutual bank and refinance it for seven years as opposed to five years. My payments would be lower. So right now I'm in a holding pattern trying to do this book, make some money and then go back to work.

Keith's History and Present Circumstances

When I divorced Janice, I got my $90,000 in equity from the house. When I moved to Brighton, the apartment was $1,000 a month. I paid for it for five years. I spent $60,000 on it and I also purchased a new Toyota Corolla with $26,000, so I only had about $4,000 left. I applied to the New Falls Apartments and I got a call from the property manager that there was an apartment available for me. But I wanted Keith to grow up in a residential area, so I turned it down. But the next year, when the property manager called, I said okay, because my money was running out and I would be able to have a Section 8 apartment. That only took 30 percent of my adjusted gross income. I had to take the apartment sight unseen. It was a garden apartment and from the outside it looked very nice; so I couldn't imagine that it wouldn't be nice inside.

I was having a problem with pediculosis at the time. It took me about two years to figure out that it was the Wellbutrin I was taking. It gave me an affinity for lice; every time I came near lice, they would get attached to my body. One night I spent about twenty-four to forty-eight hours getting lice out of my hair. One day after school, when Keith came home from school there were lice in the apartment and I didn't want him to get it. I noticed that he was getting it, so I put some of that anti-lice lotion on him and gave him a quick shower and let him out of there quickly. Janice found out that I'd put that stuff on him and she was outraged. When she went to court, she told them about it and they thought that I wasn't competent enough to be his parent.

Another time when lice were in the apartment, I put Keith in the community room. I wanted to make a call to Carolyn L. to let her know that I had a couple of references for her for orthopedic men. Her daughter needed an orthopedic man, so I gave Carolyn a quick call. Keith came to the front door of my apartment because we'd been there three or four years and by then he knew where my front door was. Again Janice was outraged. When she took me to court, she got full legal and full physical custody of Keith. I wasn't able to take him out in my car anymore with me. I went into the school once a week to try and teach him how to read for a couple of hours. All Janice was concerned with was her work and making money. She didn't care about Keith's needs. So when I went into the school to help teach him how to read, I had to be supervised. A person let me in and if we went out for a walk, I'd have to have a person walk with us. It was absolutely humiliating.

After Keith aged out of the school system at age twenty-two, he also aged out of the group residence but luckily, the Guild had gotten licensed to open adult houses and they had found a placement for him in the Billerica House. This is only about twenty minutes away from where we lived in Newton. Before the COVID hit, his mother and I were going up and going out with Keith once a week on Saturdays. We'd go out to lunch and then go for a walk and then get him an ice cream sundae. When the COVID hit, we began to see him twice a week via Zoom meetings and then later on when the COVID kind of petered out, we went back to visiting with him once a week and took him out.

Janice likes to take him home now, because it seems to be more relaxing doing that. I go get the food for lunch and she picks him up and brings him back to her house and he eats lunch and usually falls asleep on the sofa. Because you know the kind of feeling you get when you go home to your parents' house, he feels very comfortable. We wake him up after about an hour and a half and he has a walk and/or an ice cream sundae; give him music and videos and he's happy.

Janice became a creature of habit. She has this movie festival at her house on Sundays all spring, summer, fall, and winter. She does it outdoors during the nice weather in her backyard, once a week. Some of the people who come early order out and someone picks up the food. She has up to twelve to thirteen friends attending. One day when I was driving with Janice, I said to her, "You know, wouldn't it be nice of your friends to get you a gift certificate or something to show their appreciation for all the work you do for the movie festival?" She agreed and said don't tell them that it was my idea, though. She said to ask Judy to collect the money, not to collect it myself and ask Linda to go to the Dress Shop, where they both go to and buy her a gift certificate there. Well, when I confronted Judy, she said, "Oh we come all the way from Hanover. We don't come all the time and I won't be able to collect the money and then you know blah blah blah blah...." Excuses.

I met with Janice in the kitchen and she said, "Tell Heather to do it, to collect the money and then give it to Linda." So I went to Heather and she looked at me, like, "what are you talking about?" So I said it was for all the effort and work that she does to get the movie going. I said, "She deserves to be rewarded." And so Stanley went right into his pocket to contribute. Anyways at the end of the movie, Heather goes into the kitchen to give Janice the $10 and says, "This is for the movie." F****** incompetent friend...she was unbelievable. I went to Wendy, her other closest friend and she was like, "Huh, huh, huh." So it was like a traumatic experience. I told Janice that all her friends were incompetent and she said, "I know." She decided that next year she'd ask up front before the season.

So I dug up this thing called a letter of intent for Keith, in case Janice and I went out and got killed in a car accident or something. It tells everything about what he needs, what he likes, everything down to his shoe size, even where he will be buried. Janice has an estate. It's worth about $1.2 million. I figure it should be enough for him for his lifetime. He gets my Social Security when I die. Her house is worth about $800,000 and then she has about 400 to 600 thousand in financial investments. So she's worth $1.2 to $1.4 million.

I filled out most of the letter of intent and put it on a flash drive. Janice got it and she filled out the rest of it and deposited it with her lawyer. I had recommended to her to use Attorney F. in Newtonville. He made a will for her. She designated the executor of the estate to be her sister, which now has to be changed because her sister's memory is pretty much gone. So she has to change it to her brother's name. He was the backup executor anyways and then the trustees we had designated to be Wendy, her best friend, and Linda, her next best friend, and now we've decided they're too incompetent to handle it. So, we have to look into getting a professional trustee company or lawyer. She's going to contact her lawyer to find out some names for professional trustees. Wendy and Linda can observe to see what the professional trustees do, and if they don't like it, they can change that professional trustee out.

The guardian that Janice assigned is Kathleen M., a person that I had hired many years ago to be Keith's incidental teacher when he went into the living room after doing intensive therapy in the dining room. She never did much of anything, just let him play with her ring.

I'd go over to her and say why don't you teach him how to print or write and I had some templates and what not. She wouldn't do anything. So, I'm not crazy about Kathleen. I guess I'll have to go to Probate Court if Janice passes away before me. The problem with Kathleen is that she lives way up in Maine now. She used to live in Andover, Massachusetts, which wasn't too far away. Plus Kathleen is getting older too, so anyways we'll see what happens.

Janice got remarried about three or four years ago and a month after the marriage her husband passed away. He had had liver cancer when she decided to marry him and said that she wanted to give him another six months to a year of a good time. She still thinks he was her soul mate. The letter of intent was developed by some financial people, a man and a woman. The man had a child with Down syndrome and the woman had a child, I believe that's blind, so, they were like groundbreakers in this territory. They came up with the letter of intent and a team to carry on. The man's daughter is now the financial advisor there for Janice.

Janice hasn't stepped out of her second marriage. Cassie is her stepdaughter and really hasn't shown any interest in Keith. I don't think she's going to be available to do anything for Keith. She'll probably have her own kids and then have her own family and she's in another state anyways. I think she's out in the Midwest somewhere.

Janice's second husband wanted to be cremated and his ashes brought out to sea so she had this whole ceremony and she got a boat and they dumped his ashes out into the Atlantic Ocean somewhere. I told her I just wanted to be cremated and have my ashes scattered at Pemberton Point, in Nantasket, one of my favorite places to rest.

The group home that Keith lives in has four other housemates: two women and two men. As far as I can tell, he's the highest functioning of all of them. He developed epilepsy when he went into his teenage years. A lot of children with autism do develop epilepsy when they go into puberty. I got a call once from the middle school that he was attending that he wasn't feeling well and to come and pick him up. When I got there, we went to walk across the parking lot to my car and he just collapsed in the parking lot. Lo and behold there was a fire truck there because there was construction being done on the building. One of the firemen came over to me and said, "Do you want me to help you get him in the car?" and I said, "Yes, please." We put him in the car and he started turning blue so I got really scared and asked the fireman if he could call an ambulance. He said, "Yes." They put Keith in the back of the ambulance and started giving him oxygen.

I was kind of traumatized by that incident, so I reduced my visitations with Keith to once a week. My psychologist agreed with this. He said it would be good if I took a break.

So right now Keith's kind of in a holding pattern. His day program that he was going to shut down due to the Covid. He was working for Meals on Wheels a couple of times a week, the Cat Connection (a cat shelter) once per week and Buddy Dogs (a dog shelter) once a week. Also, he made these beads in the art class for necklaces and bracelets. Plus, he'd help deliver the mail from the main office to the satellite offices. They kept him quite busy at the Day Habilitation program. When COVID hit, everything got shut down. Keith couldn't go to the day program anymore and it's been a few months. The director there is having trouble hiring people because she says they don't pay enough; places like McDonald's, Home Depot, and Amazon are paying people more so she can't hire people at a competitive salary. I'm kind of fed up with her because she has too high standards and can't hire anybody. She said the earliest she could get Keith back into the program is maybe the end of December sometime, that would have been eight months ago. Recently, the Director of that program basically told us to look elsewhere. We've applied to a different place called Bridgewell Rosewood in Billerica. It's like 3/4 of a mile from his house, as opposed to a one-hour-plus bus drive some days to Newton.

He has a Development Disabilities Services (DDS) case manager named Mike R. He sent a referral packet to the Rosewood program. They determined that Keith is a good fit for their program, but they're having the same issue with finding employees. Janice and I toured the program recently and it looked ok. When we visited them about four years ago they had just started up, there were only about six clients in the program and it looked very industrial. It was in an industrial building and office building and they didn't even have a couch out in the hallway to make it look inviting and comfortable. They have a couch in one of the rooms at his previous Day Hab Program and Keith likes to lie on it and take a nap once in a while. He's gotten injured like four times now—once in the shower at the group residency; he fell down in the shower after a seizure and broke his clavicle bone. I got a chair to put in the shower so that he can sit on it while he is in the shower. A couple of other times he fell in the bathroom at the residence and got a gash above his left eye. They had to stitch it up for him at Newton-Wellesley Hospital emergency room. The doctor gave him an anesthetic to separate his body from his head while she stitched him up. Another time he cut himself over his right eye. He had a seizure and fell off the toilet and hit his head on something. Once during the day program he fell and chipped his tooth.

Janice keeps a log of his seizures in an Excel spreadsheet. She enters an antecedent type thing…like he didn't sleep well that night and so he was tired or he was sick and had a seizure. She meets with his neurologist about every three or four months. He does a blood test to see his Anti-Seizure Drug (ASD) levels and adjusts them accordingly.

When Keith has a haircut, I have to go with Janice and kind of make sure I hold his head, so he doesn't get hurt with the scissors. He's been with the same hairdresser since he was a little boy. She's very fast with the scissors and the electric razor and so she gets it done very quickly and does a decent job

When he goes to the dentist he has to go to the Tufts Dental School in Canton, which deals with special needs people. They clean his teeth every two to three months or so. He'll eventually be going to have his chipped tooth repaired again. When he goes into the Franciscan Hospital or the Shattuck, they put him out to take X-rays and repair any teeth. The last time we went in for his checkup, the dentist said she didn't see any cavities and I looked through his mouth while she was working. I didn't see any either. They looked like they're in pretty good shape. There's a referral for him to go to the Shattuck or the Franciscan hospital to have the work done.

I got a membership for him at the YMCA in Andover, Massachusetts. He can go swimming, which relaxes him, once or twice a week while he's at the group residence.

When we lived in Brighton, I had a membership at the YMCA there and I got a swimming teacher to do some swim lessons for him. I watched her for a couple of sessions and I said, "Oh, I can do that and not have to pay her." So I got in the pool and did what she had done, which was mostly like taking little plastic floating pieces like turtles, frogs, dinosaurs, etc., and throwing down the other side of the pool and having him go and retrieve them bring them back and then I threw them down the other end of the pool again and you repeat it so you kind of learn the doggy paddle on his own and I tried to teach him a hand-over -hand free-style swimming, but his arms were too strong by then; he'd resist me prompting his arms. He did learn the doggy paddle on his own.

When we moved to Newton, I had a membership for him and me at the JCC (Jewish Community Center) and I used to bring him into the workout area and I trained him on some of the Nautilus type equipment, resistance training. I used to take him swimming at the JCC too. I tried to teach him how to ice skate too. I took two plastic milk crates and I tied them together with tie wraps and he could hold on to the boxes while he skated across the ice. I was holding on to his arm while he skated, but he never learned how to walk on the skates. You have to learn how to walk before you can skate and I just had to hold on to his shoulder and I ended up with bursitis in one of my shoulders because of the stress on it.

One time, when we were at the ice-skating rink on Soldiers Field Road, I asked him if he wanted some hot chocolate. He said yah, so I was standing in the line getting him some hot chocolate. I turned around and he was gone. It scared the heck out of me. The river was next to the rink and I didn't know which way to go towards the river or down the street.

I went out to the sidewalk and I looked down the street and way down, I could see this little figure walking and I said oh my God, I hope he doesn't go out into the street. He could get killed and I ran and ran and ran until I got out of breath and then I'd stop and then I'd run some more and then I finally caught up with him. A guy had passed me on a bike. I asked him if he could go down and hold him, until I got there and he just ignored me. So I ran down. I finally caught up with him and I said oh my God. I never want to have that happen again. I can't take my eyes off him for a minute. When he's in a store he'll just walk away.

I got him into a special needs Cub Scout and then Boy Scout Troop. They did a lot of events together. They went fishing at the Concord Rod and Gun Club and Keith caught a really long fish of a particular species and he won a trophy for that species. Keith really didn't get into it. I had to hold the rod most of the time and prompted him to do it.

Carolyn L. was an organizer for the Boy Scouts but there was a Boy Scout leader who had a son who was higher functioning than Keith and the boy wanted to be a chauffeur when he grew up. There was an adaptive program for sledding and I brought Keith to it at Riverside Golf Course and they went down some of the trails on Toboggan-type sleds. I brought him to a hill in South Natick once and I had a sled for him to go down the hill with and one of the kid's sled was pointed right at Keith and I got mad because he could have hurt him. I screamed at the kid to watch out where he was going. The father was standing there and he said to me what are you talking to my son like that for? Talk to me if you want to talk to someone; if you're concerned about where my son is sledding. I never went back there, the bunch of assholes.

The Scouts were doing a project in a back room of Home Depot and suddenly I turned around and he was gone. The store put out a Code Red in the store and some people stayed at the doors to make sure that he didn't get out. They asked me what his description was and what he was wearing. They tracked him down in one of the aisles.

I call Keith's house every night around 7:30 p.m. to speak to him. I say, "Hi, Keith, Daddy here, I love you, honey. Hi, Keith. Daddy here. I love you, honey. How you doing?" Usually he says, "Good." Then I say good, I'm smiling, I'm happy that you're doing good. I blow a kiss to him through the phone. I'll say you tired and he'll usually say, "Tired." If it's late, he'll be watching a Disney Plus movie in his bedroom from his smart TV. His mother also set up a TV programmed with Disney Plus movies using Roku in the living room. So, he can select whichever movie he wants to watch. The living room has couches and chairs for all the housemates.

We keep headphones with us wherever we go. Janice programmed the chips for the headphones with music. Now we give him Bluetooth headphones with '80s music because that's what he was evaluated in middle school. They said he'd liked the '80s music more than any other. Bruce Springsteen is his favorite musician. All the chip headphones have been broken in one way or another. He usually tears off an earpiece after a while. I searched up and down for headphones that have the chip and they aren't available anymore anywhere. You probably have to go to China to get them. There's a company that's like Amazon in China that sells them. Maybe I'll ask my friend if he can navigate the Chinese website for the headphones with the chip. I gave Keith my Bluetooth headphones to use with his iPad. Janice has it all set up with Disney movies and music.

Keith was now still living at the group home. I visit him 1-2 times per week. I need to get him out of the group home. My dream is to buy a little house in the woods with 2-3 bedrooms and an attached garage.

I'll be able to write books, write songs, and do artwork. I'll train someone to do linguistics with Keith. I'll do it myself if I have to. I'm going to train this spring, summer, and fall to be able to use an ax. I'll cut down the trees on the property and set a log splitter for Keith to operate. That'll be his first chore to cut wood for the wood stove and provide the house with heat during the fall and winter. I'll teach him how to cook in the microwave mostly. That's what I was doing before. I also taught how to make hot dogs in a saucepan.

We'll have a forever house, I need to get him out of the group residence where they are mostly warehousing him.

His mother's dream is to travel the globe and socialize with her friends and go and see musicals, plays, films, and theatre. Let me have my dream and she have her dream.

So we can both be happy! She can visit him 3 weeks per year and stay in the third bedroom. We've been divorced for 21 years. I've been his primary advocate and caregiver all his life. – Amen